The
DivineArt
Of
Living

The DivineArt Of Living

Selections from
the Writings
of
Bahá'u'lláh
and
'Abdu'l-Bahá

compiled by MABEL HYDE PAINE
revised by ANNE MARIE SCHEFFER

BAHÁ'Í PUBLISHING TRUST
WILMETTE, ILLINOIS

Bahá'í Publishing Trust, Wilmette, Illinois 60091

Copyright 1944, © 1972, 1974, 1979, 1986 by the
National Spiritual Assembly of the Bahá'ís
of the United States. All rights reserved
Published 1944. New edition 1986
Printed in the United States of America
89 88 87 86   4 3 2 1

Library of Congress Cataloging in Publication Data
Main entry under title:

The Divine art of living.

  Bibliography: p.
  Includes index.
  1. Bahai Faith. I. Bahá' Alláh, 1817–1892.
II. Abdu'l-Bahá, 1844–1921. III. Paine, Mabel Hyde.
IV. Scheffer, Anne Marie, 1950–
BP370.D58 1985   297'.8982   85-6054
ISBN 0-87743-194-9

The publisher gratefully acknowledges the work of Mabel Hyde Paine, whose
pioneering efforts shaped the first edition of *The Divine Art of Living;* of Marie
Scheffer, who searched numerous books for new extracts and spent many
hours in preparing the new edition; of Richard Hill, Terrill Hayes, and Betty
J. Fisher, who shaped the manuscript for publication; of Robert Atkinson and
Betty J. Fisher, who wrote the preface; and of Frances Worthington, who
prepared the index.

Design by John Solarz

Contents

Foreword

THROUGHOUT history the great religious leaders have provided the guideposts necessary for living the life of the spirit, but they have often chosen different metaphors for describing the journey. Some forty centuries ago the psalmist wrote simply, "Lead me in the way everlasting." Jesus, however, taught His followers that "the gate is narrow and the way hard, that leads to life." Muḥammad, six centuries later, said, "Allah guideth him who seeketh His good pleasure unto paths of peace." Even though these, and other, religious traditions were all describing the "way" or the "path" with different images, they have all described the same process of spiritual development.

Today, in the revelation of Bahá'u'lláh, we have the most clearly elucidated description of the spiritual life that humanity has known. And though the path to spiritual maturity includes difficulties and hardships, 'Abdu'l-Bahá explains that personal ordeals that test the soul are really "educational and developmental." We are now beginning to understand that learning to know, love, and trust God, recognizing the purpose of this life and the life in the next world, praying and meditating daily, serving humanity, staying healthy, creating a loving home, fostering fellowship, working for peace, and assuming our role in renewing society are *all* vital aspects of spiritual development.

The Divine Art of Living, revised and expanded, addresses these topics and concerns in a new edition containing an updated selection of extracts drawn from the Bahá'í sacred writings. First issued in book form in 1944, the work grew out of a selection of passages from the holy books of several

religions—passages all centering around the theme of the
"great preoccupation of all the Messengers of God" in
guiding "mankind along the pathway to real life and truth."
The extracts, explained Mabel Hyde Paine, the compiler of the
first edition, first appeared between April 1940 and September
1941 in *World Order,* a Bahá'í magazine. The title was
borrowed from an even earlier work of the same character put
together by Mary M. Rabb.

Since *The Divine Art of Living* appeared in 1944, it has been
reprinted nine times, with a few new translations and other
revisions being made in 1960, 1974, and 1979. But as the
much-loved book neared the end of its fourth decade,
the changing interests and concerns of the world made it clear
that a new edition was needed. Moreover, a number of new
volumes of the Bahá'í sacred writings have been published
since the 1940s, and many new translations—some of familiar
passages, some never before available—have expanded our
understanding of the teachings of Bahá'u'lláh, the Prophet-
Founder of the Bahá'í Faith.

The wealth of Bahá'í writings now accessible has enhanced
this new edition of *The Divine Art of Living* in several ways.
Whereas the 1944 edition drew on some twenty sources, the
1985 edition draws on twenty-six sources. The earlier edition
contained 386 extracts and fifteen chapters, the new edition
421 extracts and sixteen chapters. A number of chapter titles
remain the same—for example, "Prayer and Meditation,"
"Faith and Certitude," and "Learning to Know and Love
God," though the contents of each has been amplified with
new materials. Other chapters from the 1944 edition have
been combined or the passages in them moved to one or
several chapters to broaden discussions of other topics. The
chapter on love and unity has become two chapters—
"Love and Fellowship," which focuses on the individual, and
"Peace and Unity," which examines relationships between
groups of people. The chapters entitled "Marriage and Family
Life" and "The Day in Which We Live" are new to the 1985
edition.

In addition, the entire book has been reorganized to reflect a more logical structure and to draw the reader from the realm of thought into the realm of practical action. The early chapters now discuss trusting in God, learning to know and love Him, and growing through the worlds of God. Then comes a cluster of chapters about the acquisition and application of spiritual qualities. Next there are chapters on the individual's relationship to increasingly larger groups of people (spouse, family, all of humanity). Finally, there is a concluding chapter on the uniqueness of the day in which we live. Thus the new edition focuses on some of the principles that can turn life into a divine art, provides examples of how to apply the principles, and raises a call to action for a truly divine life.

The impetus for the book may be found in the Bahá'í writings, for each section of *The Divine Art of Living* attempts to elucidate some of the teachings of the Bahá'í Faith, which was founded by Mírzá Ḥusayn 'Alí (1817–92), known as Bahá'u'lláh, the "Glory of God." The Bahá'í Faith's origins are intimately linked with the Bábí Faith, founded in Persia (Iran) in 1844 by Mírzá 'Alí-Muhammad (1819–50), known as the Báb, or "Gate." The Báb announced that He was not only the founder of an independent religion, but the herald of a new and far greater Prophet or Messenger of God, Who would usher in an age of peace for all mankind. In 1863 Bahá'u'lláh declared that He was the one prophesied by the Báb.

Bahá'u'lláh's teachings quickly brought Him into conflict with the Persian government and the Muslim clergy, and He was exiled from Iran to various places within the Ottoman Empire. In 1868 He was sent as a prisoner to the fortress city of Akka in the Holy Land, in the vicinity of which He passed away in 1892. In His will He appointed 'Abdu'l-Bahá (1844–1921), His eldest son, to succeed Him in leading the Bahá'í community and in interpreting the Bahá'í writings. 'Abdu'l-Bahá in turn appointed His eldest grandson, Shoghi Effendi (1897–1957), as His successor, the Guardian of the

Cause and authorized interpreter of the Bahá'í teachings.
Today the affairs of the Bahá'í world community are adminis-
tered by the Universal House of Justice, the supreme elected
council of the Bahá'í Faith.

The central teachings of the Bahá'í Faith are the oneness of
God, the oneness of religion, and the oneness of mankind.
The fundamental principles proclaimed by Bahá'u'lláh are that
some religious truths are not absolute but vary according to
the changing needs of civilization; that divine revelation is a
continuous and progressive process; that all the great religions
of the world are divine in origin; and that their missions
represent successive stages in the spiritual evolution of human
society. Since Bahá'u'lláh teaches that the purpose of religion
is the promotion of concord and unity and that religion is
the foremost agency for the achievement of peace and orderly
progress in society, the Bahá'í writings provide the outline
of institutions necessary for the establishment of peace
and world order. These include a world federation or com-
monwealth, with executive, legislative, and judiciary arms; an
international auxiliary language; a world economy; a mecha-
nism for world intercommunication; and a universal system of
currency, weights, and measures.

The Bahá'í writings also provide specific guidance that
helps Bahá'ís (followers of Bahá'u'lláh) fulfill the basic
purpose of human life—knowing and worshiping God and
"carrying forward an ever-advancing civilization"—while
they strive to bring about the unity of mankind, world peace,
and world order. For example, the Bahá'í writings call for
the fostering of a good character and the development of
spiritual qualities such as honesty, trustworthiness, compassion, and justice. These are achieved through prayer, meditation, and work done in the spirit of service to humanity—
all expressions, for Bahá'ís, of the worship of God. In the
pursuance of the Bahá'í principle of the organic oneness of
humanity, the Bahá'í writings call for the eradication of
prejudices of race, creed, class, nationality, and sex. They call
for the systematic elimination of all forms of superstition

hampering human progress and the achievement of a balance
between the material and spiritual aspects of life, both of
which rest on an understanding of the principles of an
unfettered search for truth and of the harmony of science and
religion as two facets of truth. They encourage the development of the unique talents and abilities of every individual,
through the pursuit of knowledge and the acquisition of skills,
for the practice of a trade or profession is required not only
for personal satisfaction but also for the enrichment of society
as a whole. They call for the fostering of compulsory
education for children in every land. And they call for the full
participation of both men and women in all aspects of
community life, including the elective and administrative
processes and decision making by ensuring equal opportunities, rights, and privileges for both sexes.

This new edition of *The Divine Art of Living* provides the
essential practical and spiritual guidance necessary to help us
on the journey of achieving peace and harmony in our
personal lives as well as in the world. For, as the Bahá'í
writings make clear, the goal of a unified and peaceful
humanity begins first with personal transformation, which in
turn leads to collective efforts to transform civilization. Bright
is the light that today illumines the path of spiritual
development.

It is the publisher's hope that this new edition will tempt its
readers to delve into other volumes of the Bahá'í writings
that amplify the many topics touched on in this book. For it is
through daily exploration of these volumes that individuals
can fathom the dynamics—and reap the rewards—of the
"divine art" of living.

The
DivineArt
Of
Living

1

Trusting in God

Developing Confidence in the Bounties of God

OH, trust in God! For His bounty is everlasting, and in His blessings, for they are superb. Oh! Put your faith in the Almighty, for He faileth not, and His goodness endureth forever! His sun giveth light continually, and the clouds of His mercy are full of the waters of compassion with which He waters the hearts of all who trust in Him. His refreshing breeze ever carries healing in its wings to the parched souls of men! **1**

The bounties of God will, verily, encompass a sanctified soul even as the sun's light doth the moon and stars: Be thou assured of this. **2**

Look not at thy weakness and impotence; nay, look at the power of thy Lord, which hath surrounded all regions. **3**

Trust in the assistance of thy Master,* and ask what thou wishest of the gifts of thy Lord, the Unconstrained! **4**

Let not thy hands tremble nor thy heart be disturbed, but rather be confident and firm in the love of thy Lord, the Merciful, the Clement. **5**

Trust in God, and be unmoved by either the praise or the false accusations . . . depend entirely on God. . . . **6**

---

*God.

The source of all good is trust in God, submission unto
His command, and contentment with His holy will
and pleasure.   7

Trusting God When in Difficulties

TODAY humanity is bowed down with trouble,
sorrow and grief; no one escapes. The world is wet
with tears; but, thank God, the remedy is at our doors.
Let us turn our hearts away from the world of matter and
live in the spiritual world! It alone can give us freedom!
If we are hemmed in by difficulties, we have only to
call upon God, and by His great Mercy we shall be
helped.

If sorrow and adversity visit us, let us turn our faces to
the kingdom, and heavenly consolation will be
outpoured.

If we are sick and in distress, let us implore God's
healing, and He will answer our prayer.

When our thoughts are filled with the bitterness of
this world, let us turn our eyes to the sweetness of God's
compassion, and He will send us heavenly calm! If we are
imprisoned in the material world, our spirit can soar
into the heavens, and we shall be free indeed!

When our days are drawing to a close, let us think of
the eternal worlds, and we shall be full of joy!   8

O thou handmaid aflame with the fire of God's love!
Grieve thou not over the troubles and hardships of this
nether world, nor be thou glad in times of ease and
comfort, for both shall pass away. This present life is
even as a swelling wave, or a mirage, or drifting
shadows. . . .

Know thou that the kingdom is the real world, and
this nether place is only its shadow stretching out. . . .

Rely upon God. Trust in Him. Praise Him, and
call Him continually to mind. He, verily, turneth trouble
into ease, and sorrow into solace, and toil into utter

peace. He, verily, hath dominion over all things.

If thou wouldst hearken to my words, release thyself from the fetters of whatsoever cometh to pass. Nay, rather, under all conditions thank thou thy loving Lord, and yield up thine affairs unto His Will that worketh as He pleaseth. This, verily, is better for thee than all else, in either world.   9

Never lose thy trust in God. Be thou ever hopeful, for the bounties of God never cease to flow upon man. If viewed from one perspective, they seem to decrease, but from another they are full and complete. Man is under all conditions immersed in a sea of God's blessings. Therefore, be thou not hopeless under any circumstances, but rather be firm in thy hope.   10

O thou who art turning thy face towards God! Close thine eyes to all things else, and open them to the realm of the All-Glorious. Ask whatsoever thou wishest of Him alone; seek whatsoever thou seekest from Him alone. With a look He granteth a hundred thousand hopes; with a glance He healeth a hundred thousand incurable ills; with a glimpse He layeth balm on every wound; with a nod He freeth the hearts from the shackles of grief. He doeth as He doeth, and what recourse have we? He carrieth out His Will; He ordaineth what He pleaseth. Then better for thee to bow down thy head in submission, and put thy trust in the All-Merciful Lord.   11

Relying on God Rather than on Self

THESE events* have deeper reasons. Their object and purpose is to teach man certain lessons. We are living in a day of reliance upon material conditions. Men imagine that the great size and strength of a ship, the

---

*Such as the *Titanic* disaster.

perfection of machinery or the skill of a navigator will
ensure safety, but these disasters sometimes take place
that men may know that God is the real Protector. If it
be the will of God to protect man, a little ship may
escape destruction, whereas the greatest and most per-
fectly constructed vessel with the best and most skillful
navigator may not survive a danger such as was present
on the ocean. The purpose is that the people of the
world may turn to God, the One Protector; that human
souls may rely upon His preservation and know that
He is the real safety. These events happen in order that
man's faith may be increased and strengthened. Therefore, although we feel sad and disheartened, we must
supplicate God to turn our hearts to the kingdom
and pray for these departed souls with faith in His infinite mercy so that, although they have been deprived
of this earthly life, they may enjoy a new existence in the
supreme mansions of the Heavenly Father.

Let no one imagine that these words imply that man
should not be thorough and careful in his undertakings.
God has endowed man with intelligence so that he
may safeguard and protect himself. Therefore, he must
provide and surround himself with all that scientific skill
can produce. He must be deliberate, thoughtful and
thorough in his purposes, build the best ship and provide
the most experienced captain; yet, withal, let him rely
upon God and consider God as the one Keeper. If
God protects, nothing can imperil man's safety; and if it
be not His will to safeguard, no amount of preparation
and precaution will avail. 12

The Assurance of God's Grace
and Forgiveness

PRAISE be to Thee, O my God. . . . Thou art, in
truth, He Whose mercy hath encompassed all the
worlds, and Whose grace hath embraced all that dwell on
earth and in heaven. Who is there that hath cried after

Thee, and whose prayer hath remained unanswered?
Where is he to be found who hath reached forth towards
Thee, and whom Thou hast failed to approach?   13

What outpouring flood can compare with the stream of
His all-embracing grace, and what blessing can excel
the evidences of so great and pervasive a mercy? There
can be no doubt whatever that if for one moment the
tide of His mercy and grace were to be withheld from
the world, it would completely perish. For this reason,
from the beginning that hath no beginning the portals of
divine mercy have been flung open to the face of all
created things, and the clouds of Truth will continue to
the end that hath no end to rain on the soil of human
capacity, reality and personality their favors and bounties.
Such hath been God's method continued from everlasting to everlasting.   14

O ye loved ones of God! Is there any giver save God? He
singleth out for His mercy whomsoever He willeth.
Erelong will He open before you the gates of His knowledge and fill up your hearts with His love. He will
cheer your souls with the gentle winds of His holiness
and make bright your faces with the splendors of His
lights, and exalt the memory of you amongst all peoples.
Your Lord is, verily, the Compassionate, the Merciful.
   He will come to your aid with invisible hosts, and
support you with armies of inspiration from the Concourse above; He will send unto you sweet perfumes
from the highest Paradise, and waft over you the pure
breathings that blow from the rose gardens of the Company on high. He will breathe into your hearts the
spirit of life, cause you to enter the Ark of salvation, and
reveal unto you His clear tokens and signs. Verily, is
this abounding grace.   15

Glorified art Thou, O Lord. Thou forgivest at all times
the sins of such among Thy servants as implore Thy

pardon. Wash away my sins and the sins of those who
seek Thy forgiveness at dawn, who pray to Thee in the
daytime and in the night season, who yearn after naught
save God, who offer up whatsoever God hath graciously
bestowed upon them, who celebrate Thy praise at
morn and eventide, and who are not remiss in their
duties.   16

Prayers to Increase Trust in God

O LORD! Unto Thee I repair for refuge, and toward
all Thy signs I set my heart.

O Lord! Whether traveling or at home, and in my
occupation or in my work, I place my whole trust
in Thee.

Grant me then Thy sufficing help so as to make me
independent of all things, O Thou Who art unsurpassed
in Thy mercy!

Bestow upon me my portion, O Lord, as Thou pleas-
est, and cause me to be satisfied with whatsoever Thou
hast ordained for me.

Thine is the absolute authority to command.   17

I bear witness at this moment, O my God, to my help-
lessness and Thy sovereignty, my feebleness and Thy
power. I know not that which profiteth me or harmeth
me; Thou art, verily, the All-Knowing, the All-Wise.
Do Thou decree for me, O Lord, my God, and my
Master, that which will make me feel content with
Thine eternal decree and will prosper me in every world
of Thine. Thou art, in truth, the Gracious, the
Bountiful.

Lord! Turn me not away from the ocean of Thy
wealth and the heaven of Thy mercy, and ordain for me
the good of this world and hereafter. Verily, Thou art the
Lord of the mercy-seat, enthroned in the highest; there
is none other God but Thee, the One, the All-Knowing,
the All-Wise.   18

Ordain for me, O my Lord, and for those who believe in Thee that which is deemed best for us in Thine estimation, as set forth in the Mother Book, for within the grasp of Thy hand Thou holdest the determined measures of all things.

Thy goodly gifts are unceasingly showered upon such as cherish Thy love, and the wondrous tokens of Thy heavenly bounties are amply bestowed on those who recognize Thy divine Unity. We commit unto Thy care whatsoever Thou hast destined for us, and implore Thee to grant us all the good that Thy knowledge embraceth.

Protect me, O my Lord, from every evil that Thine omniscience perceiveth, inasmuch as there is no power nor strength but in Thee, no triumph is forthcoming save from Thy presence, and it is Thine alone to command. Whatever God hath willed hath been, and that which He hath not willed shall not be.

There is no power nor strength except in God, the Most Exalted, the Most Mighty.   **19**

2

Learning to Know and Love God

The Power of Knowing and Loving God

Question.—Those who are blessed with good actions and universal benevolence, who have praiseworthy characteristics, who act with love and kindness toward all creatures, who care for the poor, and who strive to establish universal peace—what need have they of the divine teachings, of which they think indeed that they are independent? What is the condition of these people?

Answer.—Know that such actions, such efforts and such words are praiseworthy and approved, and are the glory of humanity. But these actions alone are not sufficient; they are a body of the greatest loveliness, but without spirit. No, that which is the cause of everlasting life, eternal honor, universal enlightenment, real salvation and prosperity is, first of all, the knowledge of God. It is known that the knowledge of God is beyond all knowledge, and it is the greatest glory of the human world. For in the existing knowledge of the reality of things there is material advantage, and through it outward civilization progresses; but the knowledge of God is the cause of spiritual progress and attraction, and through it the perception of truth, the exaltation of humanity, divine civilization, rightness of morals and illumination are obtained.

Second comes the love of God, the light of which shines in the lamp of the hearts of those who know God; its brilliant rays illuminate the horizon and give to man the life of the kingdom. In truth, the fruit of human existence is the love of God, for this love is the spirit of life, and the eternal bounty. If the love of God did not exist, the contingent world would be in darkness; if the love of God did not exist, the hearts of men would be dead, and deprived of the sensations of existence; if the love of God did not exist, spiritual union would be lost; if the love of God did not exist, the light of unity would not illuminate humanity; if the love of God did not exist, the East and West, like two lovers, would not embrace each other; if the love of God did not exist, division and disunion would not be changed into fraternity; if the love of God did not exist, indifference would not end in affection; if the love of God did not exist, the stranger would not become the friend. The love of the human world has shone forth from the love of God and has appeared by the bounty and grace of God.

It is clear that the reality of mankind is diverse, that opinions are various and sentiments different; and this difference of opinions, of thoughts, of intelligence, of sentiments among the human species arises from essential necessity; for the differences in the degrees of existence of creatures is one of the necessities of existence, which unfolds itself in infinite forms. Therefore, we have need of a general power which may dominate the sentiments, the opinions and the thoughts of all, thanks to which these divisions may no longer have effect, and all individuals may be brought under the influence of the unity of the world of humanity. It is clear and evident that this greatest power in the human world is the love of God. It brings the different peoples under the shadow of the tent of affection; it gives to the antagonistic and hostile nations and families the greatest love and union.

1

There are four kinds of love. The first is the love that flows from God to man; it consists of the inexhaustible graces, the divine effulgence and heavenly illumination. Through this love the world of being receives life. Through this love man is endowed with physical exist-

ence, until, through the breath of the Holy Spirit—
this same love—he receives eternal life and becomes the
image of the Living God. This love is the origin of all
the love in the world of creation.

The second is the love that flows from man to God.
This is faith, attraction to the divine, enkindlement,
progress, entrance into the kingdom of God, receiving
the bounties of God, illumination with the lights of the
kingdom. This love is the origin of all philanthropy; this
love causes the hearts of men to reflect the rays of the
Sun of Reality.

The third is the love of God towards the Self or
Identity of God. This is the transfiguration of His beauty,
the reflection of Himself in the mirror of His creation.
This is the reality of love, the Ancient Love, the Eternal
Love. Through one ray of this Love all other love exists.

The fourth is the love of man for man. The love
which exists between the hearts of believers is prompted
by the ideal of the unity of spirits. This love is attained
through the knowledge of God, so that men see the
divine love reflected in the heart. Each sees in the other
the beauty of God reflected in the soul, and finding
this point of similarity, they are attracted to one another
in love. This love will make all men the waves of one
sea; this love will make them all the stars of one heaven
and the fruits of one tree. This love will bring the
realization of true accord, the foundation of real unity.

But the love which sometimes exists between friends
is not true love because it is subject to transmutation; this
is merely fascination. As the breeze blows, the slender
trees yield. If the wind is in the east, the tree leans to the
west, and if the wind turns to the west, the tree leans to
the east. This kind of love is originated by the accidental
conditions of life. This is not love; it is merely acquaint-
anceship. It is subject to change.

Today you will see two souls apparently in close
friendship; tomorrow all this may be changed. Yesterday

they were ready to die for one another; today they shun
one another's society! This is not love; it is the yielding
of the hearts to the accidents of life. When that which
has caused this "love" to exist passes, the love passes also;
this is not in reality love.

Love is only of the four kinds that I have explained. (*a*)
The love of God towards the identity of God. Christ
has said God is Love. (*b*) The love of God for His
children—for His servants. (*c*) The love of man for God
and (*d*) the love of man for man. These four kinds of love
originate from God. These are rays from the Sun of
Reality; these are the breathings of the Holy Spirit; these
are the signs of the reality.   2

Having created the world and all that liveth and moveth
therein, He, through the direct operation of His
unconstrained and sovereign Will, chose to confer upon
man the unique distinction and capacity to know Him
and to love Him—a capacity that must needs be regarded
as the generating impulse and the primary purpose
underlying the whole of creation. . . . Upon the inmost
reality of each and every created thing He hath shed
the light of one of His names, and made it a recipient of
the glory of one of His attributes. Upon the reality of
man, however, He hath focused the radiance of all of His
names and attributes, and made it a mirror of His own
Self. Alone of all created things man hath been singled
out for so great a favor, so enduring a bounty.   3

Learning to Know God

THE energies with which the Daystar of divine
bounty and Source of heavenly guidance hath endowed the reality of man lie . . . latent within him, even
as the flame is hidden within the candle and the rays of
light are potentially present in the lamp. The radiance of
these energies may be obscured by worldly desires even

as the light of the sun can be concealed beneath the dust and dross which cover the mirror. Neither the candle nor the lamp can be lighted through their own unaided efforts, nor can it ever be possible for the mirror to free itself from its dross. It is clear and evident that until a fire is kindled the lamp will never be ignited, and unless the dross is blotted out from the face of the mirror it can never represent the image of the sun nor reflect its light and glory.

And since there can be no tie of direct intercourse to bind the one true God with His creation, and no resemblance whatever can exist between the transient and the Eternal, the contingent and the Absolute, He hath ordained that in every age and dispensation a pure and stainless Soul be made manifest in the kingdoms of earth and heaven. . . . These Essences of Detachment, these resplendent Realities are the channels of God's all-pervasive grace. Led by the light of unfailing guidance, and invested with supreme sovereignty, They are commissioned to use the inspiration of Their words, the effusions of Their infallible grace and the sanctifying breeze of Their Revelation for the cleansing of every longing heart and receptive spirit from the dross and dust of earthly cares and limitations. Then, and only then, will the Trust of God, latent in the reality of man, emerge, as resplendent as the rising Orb of divine revelation, from behind the veil of concealment, and implant the ensign of its revealed glory upon the summits of men's hearts.   4

The knowledge of the Reality of the Divinity is impossible and unattainable, but the knowledge of the Manifestations of God is the knowledge of God, for the bounties, splendors and divine attributes are apparent in Them. Therefore, if man attains to the knowledge of the Manifestations of God, he will attain to the knowledge of God; and if he be neglectful of the knowledge of the

Holy Manifestations, he will be bereft of the knowledge of God.   5

Although it is recognized that the contemporary men of learning are highly qualified in philosophy, arts and crafts, yet were anyone to observe with a discriminating eye, he would readily comprehend that most of this knowledge hath been acquired from the sages of the past, for it is they who have laid the foundation of philosophy, reared its structure and reinforced its pillars. . . . The sages aforetime acquired their knowledge from the Prophets, inasmuch as the latter were the Exponents of divine philosophy and the Revealers of heavenly mysteries.   6

The supreme cause for creating the world and all that is therein is for man to know God. In this Day whosoever is guided by the fragrance of the raiment of His mercy to gain admittance into the pristine Abode, which is the station of recognizing the Source of divine commandments and the Dayspring of His Revelation, hath everlastingly attained unto all good. Having reached this lofty station, a twofold obligation resteth upon every soul. One is to be steadfast in the Cause with such steadfastness that were all the peoples of the world to attempt to prevent him from turning to the Source of Revelation, they would be powerless to do so. The other is observance of the divine ordinances which have streamed forth from the wellspring of His heavenly propelled Pen. For man's knowledge of God cannot develop fully and adequately save by observing whatsoever hath been ordained by Him and is set forth in His heavenly Book.   7

Turn to God, supplicate humbly at His threshold, seeking assistance and confirmation, that God may rend asunder the veils that obscure your vision. Then will

your eyes be filled with illumination, face to face you
will behold the reality of God and your heart become
completely purified from the dross of ignorance, reflecting the glories and bounties of the kingdom.   8

God's Boundless Love

BEHOLD how the manifold grace of God, which is
being showered from the clouds of divine glory,
hath, in this day, encompassed the world. For whereas in
days past every lover besought and searched after his
Beloved, it is the Beloved Himself Who now is calling
His lovers and is inviting them to attain His presence.
Take heed lest ye forfeit so precious a favor; beware lest
ye belittle so remarkable a token of His grace.   9

The manifold bounties of the Lord of all beings have, at
all times, through the Manifestations of His Divine
Essence, encompassed the earth and all that dwell
therein. Not for a moment hath His grace been withheld,
nor have the showers of His loving kindness ceased to
rain upon mankind.   10

Consider to what extent the love of God makes itself
manifest. Among the signs of His love which appear in
the world are the dawning points of His Manifestations.
What an infinite degree of love is reflected by the
divine Manifestations toward mankind! For the sake of
guiding the people They have willingly forfeited Their
lives to resuscitate human hearts. They have accepted the
cross. To enable human souls to attain the supreme
degree of advancement, They have suffered during Their
limited years extreme ordeals and difficulties. If Jesus
Christ had not possessed love for the world of humanity,
surely He would not have welcomed the cross. He was
crucified for the love of mankind. Consider the infinite
degree of that love. Without love for humanity John the
Baptist would not have offered his life. It has been

likewise with all the Prophets and Holy Souls. If the Báb had not manifested love for mankind, surely He would not have offered His breast for a thousand bullets. If Bahá'u'lláh had not been aflame with love for humanity, He would not have willingly accepted forty years' imprisonment.

Observe how rarely human souls sacrifice their pleasure or comfort for others, how improbable that a man would offer his eye or suffer himself to be dismembered for the benefit of another. Yet all the divine Manifestations suffered, offered Their lives and blood, sacrificed Their existence, comfort and all They possessed for the sake of mankind. Therefore, consider how much They love. Were it not for Their love for humanity, spiritual love would be mere nomenclature. Were it not for Their illumination, human souls would not be radiant. How effective is Their love! This is a sign of the love of God, a ray of the Sun of Reality.   11

Learning to Love God

THE essence of love is for man to turn his heart to the Beloved One, and sever himself from all else but Him, and desire naught save that which is the desire of his Lord.   12

Let the flame of the love of God burn brightly within your radiant hearts. Feed it with the oil of divine guidance, and protect it within the shelter of your constancy. Guard it within the globe of trust and detachment from all else but God, so that the evil whisperings of the ungodly may not extinguish its light. O My servants! My holy, My divinely ordained Revelation may be likened unto an ocean in whose depths are concealed innumerable pearls of great price, of surpassing luster. It is the duty of every seeker to bestir himself and strive to attain the shores of this ocean, so that he may, in proportion to the eagerness of his search and the efforts he hath exerted, partake of such benefits as have been preordained in God's irrevocable and hidden Tablets.   13

The Bounties of Loving God

O SON of Man! I loved thy creation; hence I created thee. Wherefore, do thou love Me, that I may name thy name and fill thy soul with the spirit of life.   14

O Son of Being! My love is My stronghold; he that entereth therein is safe and secure, and he that turneth away shall surely stray and perish.   15

Know thou that nothing profiteth a soul save the love of the All-Merciful; nothing lighteth up a heart save the splendor that shineth from the realm of the Lord.   16

For love of God and spiritual attraction do cleanse and purify the human heart and dress and adorn it with the spotless garment of holiness; and once the heart is entirely attached to the Lord, and bound over to the Blessed Perfection, then will the grace of God be revealed.

This love is not of the body but completely of the soul. And those souls whose inner being is lit by the love of God are even as spreading rays of light, and they shine out like stars of holiness in a pure and crystalline sky. For true love, real love, is the love for God, and this is sanctified beyond the notions and imaginings of men.   17

Prayers for Attaining the Knowledge and Love of God

O MY God! O my God! This, Thy servant, hath advanced towards Thee, is passionately wandering in the desert of Thy love, walking in the path of Thy service, anticipating Thy favors, hoping for Thy bounty, relying upon Thy kingdom, and intoxicated by the wine of Thy gift. O my God! Increase the fervor of his affection for Thee, the constancy of his praise of Thee, and the ardor of his love for Thee.

Verily, Thou art the Most Generous, the Lord of grace abounding. There is no other God but Thee, the Forgiving, the Merciful.   **18**

O my Lord! O my Lord! This is a lamp lighted by the fire of Thy love and ablaze with the flame which is ignited in the tree of Thy mercy. O my Lord! Increase his enkindlement, heat and flame, with the fire which is kindled in the Sinai of Thy Manifestation. Verily, Thou art the Confirmer, the Assister, the Powerful, the Generous, the Loving.   **19**

3

Growing through the Worlds of God

The Creation and Nature of Humanity

O SON of Being! With the hands of power I made thee, and with the fingers of strength I created thee; and within thee have I placed the essence of My light.

1

According to the words of the Old Testament God has said, "Let us make man in our image, after our likeness." This indicates that man is of the image and likeness of God—that is to say, the perfections of God, the divine virtues, are reflected or revealed in the human reality. Just as the light and effulgence of the sun when cast upon a polished mirror are reflected fully, gloriously, so, likewise, the qualities and attributes of Divinity are radiated from the depths of a pure human heart. This is an evidence that man is the most noble of God's creatures. . . .

Let us now discover more specifically how he is the image and likeness of God and what is the standard or criterion by which he can be measured and estimated. This standard can be no other than the divine virtues which are revealed in him. Therefore, every man imbued with divine qualities, who reflects heavenly moralities and perfections, who is the expression of ideal and praiseworthy attributes, is, verily, in the image and likeness of God.

2

Know thou that every soul is fashioned after the nature of God, each being pure and holy at his birth. After-

20

wards, however, the individuals will vary according to what they acquire of virtues or vices in this world. Although all existent beings are in their very nature created in ranks or degrees, for capacities are various, nevertheless every individual is born holy and pure, and only thereafter may he become defiled.   3

In man there are two natures: his spiritual or higher nature and his material or lower nature. In one he approaches God; in the other he lives for the world alone. Signs of both these natures are to be found in men. In his material aspect he expresses untruth, cruelty and injustice; all these are the outcome of his lower nature. The attributes of his divine nature are shown forth in love, mercy, kindness, truth and justice, one and all being expressions of his higher nature. Every good habit, every noble quality belongs to man's spiritual nature, whereas all his imperfections and sinful actions are born of his material nature. If a man's divine nature dominates his human nature, we have a saint.

Man has the power both to do good and to do evil; if his power for good predominates and his inclinations to do wrong are conquered, then man in truth may be called a saint. But if, on the contrary, he rejects the things of God and allows his evil passions to conquer him, then he is no better than a mere animal.   4

Knowledge is a quality of man, and so is ignorance; truthfulness is a quality of man; so is falsehood; trustworthiness and treachery, justice and injustice, are qualities of man, and so forth. Briefly, all the perfections and virtues, and all the vices, are qualities of man. . . .

Man is said to be the greatest representative of God, and he is the Book of Creation because all the mysteries of beings exist in him. If he comes under the shadow of the True Educator and is rightly trained, he becomes the essence of essences, the light of lights, the spirit of spirits; he becomes the center of the divine appearances, the source of spiritual qualities, the rising-place of heavenly lights, and the receptacle of divine inspirations. If he is deprived of this education, he becomes the manifestation of satanic qualities, the sum of animal vices, and the source of all dark conditions.   5

Today all people are immersed in the world of nature. That is why thou dost see jealousy, greed, the struggle for survival, deception, hypocrisy, tyranny, oppression, disputes, strife, bloodshed, looting and pillaging, which all emanate from the world of nature. Few are those who have been freed from this darkness, who have ascended from the world of nature to the world of man, who have followed the divine teachings, have served the world of humanity, are resplendent, merciful, illumined and like unto a rose garden. Strive thine utmost to become godlike, characterized with His attributes, illumined and merciful, that thou mayest be freed from every bond and become attached at heart to the kingdom of the incomparable Lord. This is Bahá'í bounty, and this is heavenly light.   6

The Purpose of Life

I BEAR witness, O my God, that Thou hast created me to know Thee and to worship Thee. I testify, at this moment, to my powerlessness and to Thy might, to my poverty and to Thy wealth.
    There is none other God but Thee, the Help in Peril, the Self-Subsisting.   7

The purpose of God in creating man hath been, and will ever be, to enable him to know his Creator and to attain His Presence. To this most excellent aim, this supreme objective, all the heavenly Books and the divinely revealed and weighty Scriptures unequivocally bear witness.   8

Question.—"What is the purpose of our lives?"

'Abdu'l-Bahá.—"To acquire virtues. We come from the earth; why were we transferred from the mineral to the vegetable kingdom—from the plant to the animal kingdom? So that we may attain perfection in each of these kingdoms, that we may possess the best qualities of the mineral, that we may acquire the power of growing as in the plant, that we may be adorned with the instincts of the animal and possess the faculties of sight, hearing, smell, touch and taste, until from the animal kingdom we step into the world of humanity and are gifted with reason, the power of invention, and the forces of the spirit."

9

In the world of existence man has traversed successive degrees until he has attained the human kingdom. In each degree of his progression he has developed capacity for advancement to the next station and condition. While in the kingdom of the mineral he was attaining the capacity for promotion into the degree of the vegetable. In the kingdom of the vegetable he underwent preparation for the world of the animal, and from thence he has come onward to the human degree, or kingdom. Throughout this journey of progression he has ever and always been potentially man.

In the beginning of his human life man was embryonic in the world of the matrix. There he received capacity and endowment for the reality of human existence. The forces and powers necessary for this world were bestowed upon him in that limited condition. In this world he needed eyes; he received them potentially in the other. He needed ears; he obtained them there in readiness and preparation for his new existence. The powers requisite in this world were conferred upon him in the world of the matrix so that when he entered this realm of real existence he not only possessed all necessary functions and powers but found provision for his material sustenance awaiting him.

Therefore, in this world he must prepare himself for the life beyond. That which he needs in the world of the kingdom must be obtained here. Just as he prepared himself in the world of the matrix by acquiring forces necessary in this sphere of existence, so, likewise, the indispensable forces of the divine existence must be potentially attained in this world.

What is he in need of in the kingdom which transcends the life and limitation of this mortal sphere? That world beyond is a world of sanctity and radiance; therefore, it is necessary that in this world he should acquire these divine attributes. In that world there is need of spirituality, faith, assurance, the knowledge and love of God. These he must attain in this world so that after his ascension from the earthly to the heavenly kingdom he shall find all that is needful in that eternal life ready for him.

That divine world is manifestly a world of lights; therefore, man has need of illumination here. That is a world of love; the love of God is essential. It is a world of perfections; virtues, or perfections, must be acquired. That world is vivified by the breaths of the Holy Spirit; in this world we must seek them. That is the kingdom of everlasting life; it must be attained during this vanishing existence.

By what means can man acquire these things? How shall he obtain these merciful gifts and powers? First, through the knowledge of God. Second, through the love of God. Third, through faith. Fourth, through philanthropic deeds. Fifth, through self-sacrifice. Sixth, through severance from this world. Seventh, through sanctity and holiness. Unless he acquires these forces and attains to these requirements, he will surely be deprived of the life that is eternal. But if he possesses the knowledge of God, becomes ignited through the fire of the love of God, witnesses the great and mighty signs of the kingdom, becomes the cause of love among mankind and lives in the utmost state of sanctity and

holiness, he shall surely attain to second birth, be baptized
by the Holy Spirit and enjoy everlasting existence.   10

Attaining the Kingdom of God

THERE is . . . [a] Spirit, which may be termed the
divine, to which Jesus Christ refers when He
declares that man must be born of its quickening and
baptized with its living fire. Souls deprived of that Spirit
are accounted as dead, though they are possessed of the
human spirit. Jesus Christ has pronounced them dead
inasmuch as they have no portion of the divine Spirit. He
says, "Let the dead bury their dead." In another instance
He declares, "That which is born of the flesh is flesh;
and that which is born of the Spirit is spirit." By this He
means that souls, though alive in the human kingdom,
are nevertheless dead if devoid of this particular spirit of
divine quickening. They have not partaken of the
divine life of the higher kingdom, for the soul which
partakes of the power of the divine Spirit is, verily,
living.   11

O Son of Dust! Blind thine eyes, that thou mayest behold
My beauty; stop thine ears, that thou mayest hearken
unto the sweet melody of My voice; empty thyself of all
learning, that thou mayest partake of My knowledge;
and sanctify thyself from riches, that thou mayest obtain
a lasting share from the ocean of My eternal wealth.
Blind thine eyes, that is, to all save My beauty; stop thine
ears to all save My word; empty thyself of all learning
save the knowledge of Me; that with a clear vision, a
pure heart and an attentive ear thou mayest enter the
court of My holiness.   12

O My Servant! Purge thy heart from malice and, inno-
cent of envy, enter the divine court of holiness.   13

Thou didst ask whether, at the advent of the kingdom of

God, every soul was saved. The Sun of Truth hath
shone forth in splendor over all the world, and its luminous rising is man's salvation and his eternal life—but
only he is of the saved who hath opened wide the eye of
his discernment and beheld that glory.   14

Entrance into the kingdom is through the love of God,
through detachment, through holiness and chastity,
through truthfulness, purity, steadfastness, faithfulness
and the sacrifice of life.
    . . . For those who believe in God, who have love of
God, and faith, life is excellent—that is, it is eternal; but
to those souls who are veiled from God, although they
have life, it is dark, and in comparison with the life
of believers it is nonexistence.   15

All praise be unto Thee, O Thou besides Whom there is
none other God. Graciously enable me to ascend unto
Thee, to be granted the honor of dwelling in Thy
nearness and to have communion with Thee alone. No
God is there but Thee.   16

The Challenges of Living in
the Spiritual Kingdom

FROM amongst all mankind hath He chosen you, and
your eyes have been opened to the light of guidance
and your ears attuned to the music of the Company
above; and blessed by abounding grace, your hearts and
souls have been born into new life. Thank ye and praise
ye God that the hand of infinite bestowals hath set
upon your heads this gem-studded crown, this crown
whose lustrous jewels will forever flash and sparkle down
all the reaches of time.
    To thank Him for this, make ye a mighty effort, and
choose for yourselves a noble goal. Through the power of
faith, obey ye the teachings of God, and let all your
actions conform to His laws.   17

O ye beloved of God, offer up thanks that ye have, in the day of the dawning, turned your faces unto the Light of the World and beheld its splendors. Ye have received a share of the light of truth; ye have enjoyed a portion of those blessings that endure forever; and therefore, as a returning of thanks for this bounty, rest ye not for a moment, sit ye not silent, carry to men's ears the glad tidings of the kingdom, spread far and wide the Word of God.

Act in accordance with the counsels of the Lord: that is, rise up in such wise, and with such qualities, as to endow the body of this world with a living soul, and to bring this young child, humanity, to the stage of adulthood. So far as ye are able, ignite a candle of love in every meeting, and with tenderness rejoice and cheer ye every heart. Care for the stranger as for one of your own; show to alien souls the same loving kindness ye bestow upon your faithful friends. Should any come to blows with you, seek to be friends with him; should any stab you to the heart, be ye a healing salve unto his sores; should any taunt and mock at you, meet him with love. Should any heap his blame upon you, praise him; should he offer you a deadly poison, give him the choicest honey in exchange; and should he threaten your life, grant him a remedy that will heal him evermore. Should he be pain itself, be ye his medicine; should he be thorns, be ye his roses and sweet herbs. Perchance such ways and words from you will make this darksome world turn bright at last; will make this dusty earth turn heavenly, this devilish prison place become a royal palace of the Lord—so that war and strife will pass and be no more, and love and trust will pitch their tents on the summits of the world. Such is the essence of God's admonitions; such in sum are the teachings for the Dispensation of Bahá.   18

O ye peoples of the kingdom! How many a soul expended all its span of life in worship, endured the mortifica-

tion of the flesh, longed to gain an entry into the
Kingdom, and yet failed, while ye, with neither toil nor
pain nor self-denial, have won the prize and entered in.

It is even as in the time of the Messiah, when the
Pharisees and the pious were left without a portion,
while Peter, John and Andrew, given neither to pious
worship nor ascetic practice, won the day. Wherefore,
thank ye God for setting upon your heads the crown of
glory everlasting, for granting unto you this immeasur-
able grace.

The time hath come when, as a thank-offering for this
bestowal, ye should grow in faith and constancy as day
followeth day, and should draw ever nearer to the Lord
your God, becoming magnetized to such a degree, and so
aflame, that your holy melodies in praise of the Beloved
will reach upward to the Company on high; and that
each one of you, even as a nightingale in this rose garden
of God, will glorify the Lord of Hosts, and become the
teacher of all who dwell on earth.   19

Verily, God has chosen you for His love and knowledge;
God has chosen you for the worthy service of unifying
mankind; God has chosen you for the purpose of investigating reality and promulgating international peace;
God has chosen you for the progress and development of
humanity, for spreading and proclaiming true education,
for the expression of love toward your fellow creatures
and the removal of prejudice; God has chosen you to
blend together human hearts and give light to the
human world. The doors of His generosity are wide,
wide open to us; but we must be attentive, alert and
mindful, occupied with service to all mankind, appreciating the bestowals of God and ever conforming to His
will.   20

Achieving True Happiness

O SON of Spirit! With the joyful tidings of light I
hail thee: rejoice!   21

O Son of Man! Rejoice in the gladness of thine heart, that thou mayest be worthy to meet Me and to mirror forth My beauty. 22

Know thou that there are two kinds of happiness—spiritual and material.

As to material happiness, it never exists; nay, it is but imagination, an image reflected in mirrors, a specter and shadow. Consider the nature of material happiness. It is something which but slightly removes one's afflictions; yet the people imagine it to be joy, delight, exultation and blessing. All the material blessings, including food, drink, etc., tend only to allay thirst, hunger and fatigue. They bestow no delight on the mind nor pleasure on the soul; nay, they furnish only the bodily wants. So this kind of happiness has no real existence.

As to spiritual happiness, this is the true basis of the life of man because life is created for happiness, not for sorrow; for pleasure, not for grief. Happiness is life; sorrow is death. Spiritual happiness is life eternal. This is a light which is not followed by darkness. This is an honor which is not followed by shame. This is a life that is not followed by death. This is an existence that is not followed by annihilation. This great blessing and precious gift is obtained by man only through the guidance of God. . . .

This happiness is the fundamental basis from which man is created, worlds are originated, the contingent beings have existence and the world of God appears like unto the appearance of the sun at midday.

This happiness is but the love of God. . . .

Were it not for this happiness the world of existence would not have been created. 23

Happiness consisteth of two kinds: physical and spiritual. The physical happiness is limited; its utmost duration is one day, one month, one year. It hath no result. Spiritual happiness is eternal and unfathomable. This kind of

happiness appeareth in one's soul with the love of God
and suffereth one to attain to the virtues and perfections
of the world of humanity. Therefore, endeavor as much
as thou art able in order to illumine the lamp of thy
heart by the light of love.   24

You see all round you proofs of the inadequacy of
material things—how joy, comfort, peace and consolation are not to be found in the transitory things of
the world. Is it not then foolishness to refuse to seek
these treasures where they may be found? The doors of
the spiritual kingdom are open to all, and without is
absolute darkness.   25

Mankind is submerged in the sea of materialism and
occupied with the affairs of this world. They have no
thought beyond earthly possessions and manifest no
desire save the passions of this fleeting, mortal existence.
Their utmost purpose is the attainment of material
livelihood, physical comforts and worldly enjoyments
such as constitute the happiness of the animal world
rather than the world of man.
    The honor of man is through the attainment of the
knowledge of God; his happiness is from the love of
God; his joy is in the glad tidings of God; his greatness is
dependent upon his servitude to God. The highest
development of man is his entrance into the divine kingdom, and the outcome of this human existence is the
nucleus and essence of eternal life. If man is bereft of the
divine bestowals and if his enjoyment and happiness are
restricted to his material inclinations, what distinction or
difference is there between the animal and himself? In
fact, the animal's happiness is greater, for its wants
are fewer and its means of livelihood easier to acquire.
Although it is necessary for man to strive for material
needs and comforts, his real need is the acquisition of the
bounties of God. If he is bereft of divine bounties,
spiritual susceptibilities and heavenly glad tidings, the

life of man in this world has not yielded any worthy
fruit. While possessing physical life, he should lay hold
of the life spiritual, and together with bodily comforts
and happiness, he should enjoy divine pleasures and
content. Then is man worthy of the title man; then will
he be after the image and likeness of God, for the image
of the Merciful consists of the attributes of the heavenly
kingdom. If no fruits of the kingdom appear in the
garden of his soul, man is not in the image and likeness
of God, but if those fruits are forthcoming, he becomes
the recipient of ideal bestowals and is enkindled with the
fire of the love of God.   26

The happiness and greatness, the rank and station, the
pleasure and peace, of an individual have never consisted
in his personal wealth, but rather in his excellent
character, his high resolve, the breadth of his learning,
and his ability to solve difficult problems.   27

Happy are the wise that have recognized the straight
path of God and turned unto His kingdom; happy are
the glad and sincere, the lamps of whose hearts burn
with the knowledge of the All-Merciful and are protected by self-abnegation from the rough winds of test and
sorrows; happy are the brave whose hearts the power
of the oppressor cannot daunt; happy are the clear-
sighted that have learned to distinguish the transitory
from the eternal, that have turned their faces to the
Imperishable and are named among the immortals in the
realm of power and glory. . . .   28

Living a Fruitful Life

WHAT are the fruits of the human world? They are
the spiritual attributes which appear in man. If
man is bereft of those attributes, he is like a fruitless tree.
One whose aspiration is lofty and who has developed
self-reliance will not be content with a mere animal

existence. He will seek the divine kingdom; he will long
to be in heaven although he still walks the earth in his
material body, and though his outer visage be physical,
his face of inner reflection will become spiritual and
heavenly. Until this station is attained by man, his life
will be utterly devoid of real outcomes. The span of his
existence will pass away in eating, drinking and sleeping,
without eternal fruits, heavenly traces or illumination—
without spiritual potency, everlasting life or the lofty
attainments intended for him during his pilgrimage
through the human world.   29

Man is like unto a tree. If he be adorned with fruit, he
hath been and will ever be worthy of praise and com-
mendation. Otherwise, a fruitless tree is but fit for fire.
The fruits of the human tree are exquisite, highly
desired and dearly cherished. Among them are upright
character, virtuous deeds and a goodly utterance. The
springtime for earthly trees occurreth once every year,
while the one for human trees appeareth in the Days of
God—exalted be His glory. Were the trees of men's lives
to be adorned in this divine springtime with the fruits
that have been mentioned, the effulgence of the light of
justice would, of a certainty, illumine all the dwellers
of the earth, and everyone would abide in tranquillity
and contentment beneath the sheltering shadow of Him
Who is the Object of all mankind.   30

Expend your every breath of life in this great Cause and
dedicate all your days to the service of Bahá, so that in
the end, safe from loss and deprivation, ye will inherit
the heaped-up treasures of the realms above. For the days
of a man are full of peril, and he cannot rely on so
much as a moment more of life; and still the people, who
are even as a wavering mirage of illusions, tell themselves
that in the end they shall reach the heights. Alas for
them! The men of bygone times hugged these same

fancies to their breasts, until a wave flicked over them and they returned to dust, and they found themselves excluded and bereft—all save those souls who had freed themselves from self and had flung away their lives in the pathway of God. Their bright star shone out in the skies of ancient glory, and the handed-down memories of all the ages are the proof of what I say.

Wherefore, rest ye neither day nor night, and seek no ease. Tell ye the secrets of servitude, follow the pathway of service, till ye attain the promised succor that cometh from the realms of God.   31

O Son of Being! Bring thyself to account each day ere thou art summoned to a reckoning; for death, unheralded, shall come upon thee, and thou shalt be called to give account for thy deeds.   32

Every soul seeketh an object and cherisheth a desire, and day and night striveth to attain his aim. One craveth riches, another thirsteth for glory and still another yearneth for fame, for art, for prosperity and the like. Yet finally all are doomed to loss and disappointment. One and all they leave behind them all that is theirs and empty-handed hasten to the realm beyond, and all their labors shall be in vain. To dust they shall all return, denuded, depressed, disheartened and in utter despair.

But, praised be the Lord, thou art engaged in that which secureth for thee a gain that shall eternally endure; and that is naught but thine attraction to the kingdom of God, thy faith, and thy knowledge, the enlightenment of thine heart, and thine earnest endeavor to promote the divine teachings.

Verily this gift is imperishable, and this wealth is a treasure from on high!   33

True loss is for him whose days have been spent in utter ignorance of his self.   34

The fleeting hours of man's life on earth pass swiftly by, and the little that still remaineth shall come to an end, but that which endureth and lasteth for evermore is the fruit that man reapeth from his servitude at the Divine Threshold. Behold the truth of this saying, how abundant and glorious are the proofs thereof in the world of being! 35

4

The Realm of Immortality

The Nature of the Soul

THOU has asked Me concerning the nature of the
soul. Know, verily, that the soul is a sign of God, a
heavenly gem whose reality the most learned of men
hath failed to grasp, and whose mystery no mind,
however acute, can ever hope to unravel. It is the first
among all created things to declare the excellence of its
Creator, the first to recognize His glory, to cleave to
His truth, and to bow down in adoration before Him. If
it be faithful to God, it will reflect His light, and will,
eventually, return unto Him. If it fail, however, in its
allegiance to its Creator, it will become a victim to self
and passion, and will, in the end, sink in their depths. 1

Know thou, of a truth, that if the soul of man hath
walked in the ways of God, it will, assuredly, return and
be gathered to the glory of the Beloved. . . . It shall
attain a station such as no pen can depict, or tongue
describe. The soul that hath remained faithful to the
Cause of God, and stood unwaveringly firm in His Path
shall, after his ascension, be possessed of such power that
all the worlds which the Almighty hath created can
benefit through him. Such a soul provideth, at the
bidding of the Ideal King and Divine Educator, the pure
leaven that leaveneth the world of being, and furnisheth
the power through which the arts and wonders of the
world are made manifest. Consider how meal needeth
leaven to be leavened with. Those souls that are the

symbols of detachment are the leaven of the world. Meditate on this, and be of the thankful.   2

Punishments and Rewards

IT IS evident that the loftiest mansions in the Realm of Immortality have been ordained as the habitation of them that have truly believed in God and in His signs. Death can never invade that holy seat.   3

The immortality of the spirit is mentioned in the Holy Books; it is the fundamental basis of the divine religions. Now punishments and rewards are said to be of two kinds: first, the rewards and punishments of this life; second, those of the other world. But the paradise and hell of existence are found in all the worlds of God, whether in this world or in the spiritual, heavenly worlds. Gaining these rewards is the gaining of eternal life.   4

The rewards of the other world are the eternal life which is clearly mentioned in all the Holy Books, the divine perfections, the eternal bounties and everlasting felicity. The rewards of the other world are the perfections and the peace obtained in the spiritual worlds after leaving this world, while the rewards of this life are the real luminous perfections which are realized in this world, and which are the cause of eternal life, for they are the very progress of existence. . . . The rewards of the other world are peace, the spiritual graces, the various spiritual gifts in the kingdom of God, the gaining of the desires of the heart and the soul, and the meeting of God in the world of eternity. In the same way the punishments of the other world—that is to say, the torments of the other world—consist in being deprived of the special divine blessings and the absolute bounties, and falling into the lowest degrees of existence. He who is deprived of these divine favors, although he continues after death, is considered as dead by the people of truth.

5

The Release of the Spirit

O SON of Man! Thou art My dominion and My dominion perisheth not; wherefore fearest thou thy perishing? Thou art My light and My light shall never be extinguished; why dost thou dread extinction? Thou art My glory and My glory fadeth not; thou art My robe and My robe shall never be outworn. Abide then in thy love for Me, that thou mayest find Me in the realm of glory.

6

To consider that after the death of the body the spirit perishes is like imagining that a bird in a cage will be destroyed if the cage is broken, though the bird has nothing to fear from the destruction of the cage. Our body is like the cage, and the spirit is like the bird. We see that without the cage this bird flies in the world of sleep; therefore, if the cage becomes broken, the bird will continue and exist. Its feelings will be even more powerful, its perceptions greater, and its happiness increased.

7

A friend asked: "How should one look forward to death?"

'Abdu'l-Bahá answered: "How does one look forward to the goal of any journey? With hope and with expectation. It is even so with the end of this earthly journey. In the next world, man will find himself freed from many of the disabilities under which he now suffers. Those who have passed on through death have a sphere of their own. It is not removed from ours; their work, the work of the kingdom, is ours; but it is sanctified from what we call 'time and place.' Time with us is measured

by the sun. When there is no more sunrise, and no more sunset, that kind of time does not exist for man. Those who have ascended have different attributes from those who are still on earth, yet there is no real separation.

"In prayer there is a mingling of station, a mingling of condition. Pray for them as they pray for you!" 8

Life in the Next World

DEATH proffereth unto every confident believer the cup that is life indeed. It bestoweth joy, and is the bearer of gladness. It conferreth the gift of everlasting life. 9

O Son of Spirit! With the joyful tidings of light I hail thee: rejoice! To the court of holiness I summon thee; abide therein that thou mayest live in peace forevermore. 10

It is clear and evident that all men shall, after their physical death, estimate the worth of their deeds, and realize all that their hands have wrought. . . . They that are the followers of the one true God shall, the moment they depart out of this life, experience such joy and gladness as would be impossible to describe, while they that live in error shall be seized with such fear and trembling, and shall be filled with such consternation, as nothing can exceed. Well is it with him that hath quaffed the choice and incorruptible wine of faith through the gracious favor and the manifold bounties of Him Who is the Lord of all Faiths. . . . 11

When the human soul soareth out of this transient heap of dust and riseth into the world of God, then veils will fall away, and verities will come to light, and all things unknown before will be made clear, and hidden truths be understood.

Consider how a being, in the world of the womb, was
deaf of ear and blind of eye, and mute of tongue; how
he was bereft of any perceptions at all. But once out of
that world of darkness, he passed into this world of light,
then his eye saw, his ear heard, his tongue spoke. In the
same way, once he hath hastened away from this mortal
place into the kingdom of God, then he will be born
in the spirit; then the eye of his perception will open, the
ear of his soul will hearken, and all the truths of which
he was ignorant before will be made plain and clear.   12

As to thy question regarding discoveries made by the
soul after it hath put off its human form: Certainly, that
world is a world of perceptions and discoveries, for the
interposed veil will be lifted away and the human spirit
will gaze upon souls that are above, below, and on a
par with itself. It is similar to the condition of a human
being in the womb, where his eyes are veiled, and all
things are hidden away from him. Once he is born out of
the uterine world and entereth this life, he findeth it,
with relation to that of the womb, to be a place of
perceptions and discoveries, and he observeth all things
through his outer eye. In the same way, once he hath
departed this life, he will behold in that world whatsoever was hidden from him here: But there he will
look upon and comprehend all things with his inner eye.
There will he gaze on his fellows and his peers, and
those in the ranks above him, and those below. As for
what is meant by the equality of souls in the all-highest
realm, it is this: The souls of the believers, at the time
when they first become manifest in the world of the
body, are equal, and each is sanctified and pure. In this
world, however, they will begin to differ one from
another, some achieving the highest station, some a
middle one, others remaining at the lowest stage of
being. Their equal status is at the beginning of their
existence; the differentiation followeth their passing
away.   13

. . . And know thou for a certainty that in the divine
worlds the spiritual beloved ones will recognize one another, and will seek union with each other, but a spiritual
union. Likewise a love that one may have entertained for
anyone will not be forgotten in the world of the kingdom, nor wilt thou forget there the life that thou hadst
in the material world.   14

It is even possible that the condition of those who have
died in sin and unbelief may become changed—that is to
say, they may become the object of pardon through the
bounty of God, not through His justice—for bounty
is giving without desert, and justice is giving what
is deserved. As we have power to pray for these souls
here, so likewise we shall possess the same power in the
other world, which is the kingdom of God. Are not
all the people in that world the creatures of God? Therefore, in that world also they can make progress. As here
they can receive light by their supplications, there also
they can plead for forgiveness and receive light through
entreaties and supplications. Thus as souls in this world,
through the help of the supplications, the entreaties
and the prayers of the holy ones, can acquire development, so is it the same after death. Through their own
prayers and supplications they can also progress, more
especially when they are the object of the intercession of
the Holy Manifestations.   15

Consolation for the Bereaved

WHEN I consider this calamity* in another aspect, I
am consoled by the realization that the worlds
of God are infinite; that though they were deprived
of this existence, they have other opportunities in the life
beyond, even as Christ has said, "In my Father's house

---

*The sinking of the *Titanic,* 1912.

are many mansions." They were called away from the
temporary and transferred to the eternal; they abandoned
this material existence and entered the portals of the
spiritual world. Foregoing the pleasures and comforts of
the earthly, they now partake of a joy and happiness far
more abiding and real, for they have hastened to the
kingdom of God. The mercy of God is infinite, and it is
our duty to remember these departed souls in our prayers
and supplications that they may draw nearer and nearer
to the Source itself.

These human conditions may be likened to the matrix
of the mother from which a child is to be born into the
spacious outer world. At first the infant finds it very
difficult to reconcile itself to its new existence. It cries as
if not wishing to be separated from its narrow abode
and imagining that life is restricted to that limited space.
It is reluctant to leave its home, but nature forces it into
this world. Having come into its new conditions, it finds
that it has passed from darkness into a sphere of
radiance; from gloomy and restricted surroundings it has
been transferred to a spacious and delightful environ-
ment. Its nourishment was the blood of the mother; now
it finds delicious food to enjoy. Its new life is filled with
brightness and beauty; it looks with wonder and delight
upon the mountains, meadows and fields of green, the
rivers and fountains, the wonderful stars; it breathes the
life-quickening atmosphere; and then it praises God
for its release from the confinement of its former condition and attainment to the freedom of a new realm.
This analogy expresses the relation of the temporal world
to the life hereafter—the transition of the soul of man
from darkness and uncertainty to the light and reality of
the eternal Kingdom. At first it is very difficult to
welcome death, but after attaining its new condition the
soul is grateful, for it has been released from the bondage
of the limited to enjoy the liberties of the unlimited. It
has been freed from a world of sorrow, grief and trials to

live in a world of unending bliss and joy. The phenome-
nal and physical have been abandoned in order that it
may attain the opportunities of the ideal and spiritual.
Therefore, the souls of those who have passed away from
earth and completed their span of mortal pilgrimage in
the *Titanic* disaster have hastened to a world superior
to this. They have soared away from these conditions of
darkness and dim vision into the realm of light. These
are the only considerations which can comfort and
console those whom they have left behind.   16

O ye two patient souls! Your letter was received. The
death of that beloved youth and his separation from you
have caused the utmost sorrow and grief; for he winged
his flight in the flower of his age and the bloom of his
youth to the heavenly nest. But he hath been freed from
this sorrow-stricken shelter and hath turned his face
toward the everlasting nest of the kingdom, and, being
delivered from a dark and narrow world, hath hastened
to the sanctified realm of light; therein lieth the consolation of our hearts.

The inscrutable divine wisdom underlieth such
heartrending occurrences. It is as if a kind gardener
transferreth a fresh and tender shrub from a confined
place to a wide open area. This transfer is not the cause
of the withering, the lessening or the destruction of that
shrub; nay, on the contrary, it maketh it to grow and
thrive, acquire freshness and delicacy, become green and
bear fruit. This hidden secret is well known to the
gardener, but those souls who are unaware of this bounty
suppose that the gardener, in his anger and wrath, hath
uprooted the shrub. Yet to those who are aware, this
concealed fact is manifest, and this predestined decree is
considered a bounty. Do not feel grieved or disconsolate,
therefore, at the ascension of that bird of faithfulness;
nay, under all circumstances pray for that youth, supplicating for him forgiveness and the elevation of his
station.   17

Thou hast written of the severe calamity that hath
befallen thee—the death of thy respected husband. That
honorable man hath been so subjected to the stress and
strain of this world that his greatest wish was for deliver-
ance from it. Such is this mortal abode: a storehouse of
afflictions and suffering. It is ignorance that binds man to
it, for no comfort can be secured by any soul in this
world, from monarch down to the most humble com-
moner. If once this life should offer a man a sweet cup, a
hundred bitter ones will follow; such is the condition
of this world. The wise man, therefore, doth not attach
himself to this mortal life and doth not depend upon
it; at some moments, even, he eagerly wisheth for death
that he may thereby be freed from these sorrows and
afflictions. Thus it is seen that some, under extreme
pressure of anguish, have committed suicide.

As to thy husband, rest assured. He will be immersed
in the ocean of pardon and forgiveness and will become
the recipient of bounty and favor. Strive thine utmost
to give his child a Bahá'í training so that when he
attaineth maturity he may be merciful, illumined and
heavenly.   18

Prayers for the Departed

O MY God! O Thou forgiver of sins, bestower of
gifts, dispeller of afflictions!

Verily, I beseech Thee to forgive the sins of such as
have abandoned the physical garment and have ascended
to the spiritual world.

O my Lord! Purify them from trespasses, dispel their
sorrows, and change their darkness into light. Cause
them to enter the garden of happiness, cleanse them with
the most pure water, and grant them to behold Thy
splendors on the loftiest mount.   19

O my God! O my God! Verily, Thy servant, humble
before the majesty of Thy divine supremacy, lowly at the

door of Thy oneness, hath believed in Thee and in Thy verses, hath testified to Thy word, hath been enkindled with the fire of Thy love, hath been immersed in the depths of the ocean of Thy knowledge, hath been attracted by Thy breezes, hath relied upon Thee, hath turned his face to Thee, hath offered his supplications to Thee, and hath been assured of Thy pardon and forgiveness. He hath abandoned this mortal life and hath flown to the kingdom of immortality, yearning for the favor of meeting Thee.

O Lord, glorify his station, shelter him under the pavilion of Thy supreme mercy, cause him to enter Thy glorious paradise, and perpetuate his existence in Thine exalted rose garden, that he may plunge into the sea of light in the world of mysteries.

Verily, Thou art the Generous, the Powerful, the Forgiver and the Bestower.   20

5

Prayer and Meditation

The Benefits of Prayer

THE state of prayer is the best of conditions, for man is then associating with God.   1

Only in the remembrance of God can the heart find rest.   2

Remembrance of Me cleanseth all things from defilement, could ye but perceive it.   3

Remembrance of Me is a healing medicine to the souls and a light to the hearts of men.   4

Another correspondent asked: "Why pray? What is the wisdom thereof, for God has established everything and executes all affairs after the best order—therefore, what is the wisdom in beseeching and supplicating and in stating one's wants and seeking help?"

'Abdu'l-Bahá replied: "Know thou, verily, it is becoming in a weak one to supplicate to the Strong One, and it behooveth a seeker of bounty to beseech the Glorious Bountiful One. When one supplicates to his Lord, turns to Him and seeks bounty from His Ocean, this supplication brings light to his heart, illumination to his sight, life to his soul and exaltation to his being.

"During thy supplications to God and thy reciting, 'Thy Name is my healing,' consider how thine heart is cheered, thy soul delighted by the spirit of the love of God, and thy mind attracted to the kingdom of God! By these attractions one's ability and capacity increase. When the vessel is enlarged, the water increases; and when the thirst grows, the bounty of the cloud becomes agreeable to the taste of man. This is the mystery of supplication and the wisdom of stating one's wants." 5

If one friend loves another, is it not natural that he should wish to say so? Though he knows that that friend is aware of his love, does he still not wish to tell him of it? . . . It is true that God knows the wishes of all hearts; but the impulse to pray is a natural one, springing from man's love to God.

. . . Prayer need not be in words, but rather in thought and action. But if this love and this desire are lacking, it is useless to try to force them. Words without love mean nothing. If a person talks to you as an unpleasant duty, finding neither love nor enjoyment in the meeting, do you wish to converse with him? 6

O thou spiritual friend! Thou hast asked the wisdom of prayer. Know thou that prayer is indispensable and obligatory, and man under no pretext whatsoever is excused from performing the prayer unless he be mentally unsound, or an insurmountable obstacle prevent him. The wisdom of prayer is this: that it causeth a connection between the servant and the True One, because in that state man with all heart and soul turneth his face towards His Highness the Almighty, seeking His association and desiring His love and compassion. The greatest happiness for a lover is to converse with his beloved, and the greatest gift for a seeker is to become familiar with the object of his longing; that is why with every soul who is attracted to the kingdom of God, his greatest hope is to find an opportunity to entreat and supplicate before his Beloved, appeal for His mercy and grace and be immersed in the ocean of His utterance, goodness and generosity.

Beside all this, prayer and fasting is the cause of awakening and mindfulness and conducive to protection and preservation from tests. 7

Intone, O My servant, the verses of God that have been received by thee, as intoned by them who have drawn nigh unto Him, that the sweetness of thy melody may kindle thine own soul, and attract the hearts of all men. Whoso reciteth, in the privacy of his chamber, the verses revealed by God, the scattering angels of the Almighty shall scatter abroad the fragrance of the words uttered by his mouth, and shall cause the heart of every righteous man to throb. Though he may, at first, remain unaware of its effect, yet the virtue of the grace vouchsafed unto him must needs sooner or later exercise its influence upon his soul.   8

O Son of Being! Make mention of Me on My earth, that in My heaven I may remember thee; thus shall Mine eyes and thine be solaced.   9

Developing a Prayerful Attitude

O SON of Glory! Be swift in the path of holiness, and enter the heaven of communion with Me. Cleanse thy heart with the burnish of the spirit, and hasten to the court of the Most High.   10

Set all thy hope in God, and cleave tenaciously to His unfailing mercy.   11

Depend thou upon God. Forsake thine own will and cling to His; set aside thine own desires and lay hold of His. . . .   12

True remembrance is to make mention of the Lord, the All-Praised, and forget aught else beside Him.   13

The reason why privacy hath been enjoined in moments of devotion is this, that thou mayest give thy best attention to the remembrance of God, that thy heart may at all times be animated with His Spirit, and not be shut

out as by a veil from thy Best Beloved. Let not thy
tongue pay lip service in praise of God while thy heart
be not attuned to the exalted Summit of Glory, and
the Focal Point of communion.   14

Worship thou God in such wise that if thy worship lead
thee to the fire, no alteration in thine adoration would be
produced, and so likewise if thy recompense should be
paradise. Thus and thus alone should be the worship
which befitteth the one True God. Shouldst thou worship
Him because of fear, this would be unseemly in the
sanctified Court of His presence, and could not be
regarded as an act by thee dedicated to the Oneness of
His Being. Or if thy gaze should be on paradise, and
thou shouldst worship Him while cherishing such
a hope, thou wouldst make God's creation a partner with
Him, notwithstanding the fact that paradise is desired
by men.

Fire and paradise both bow down and prostrate themselves before God. That which is worthy of His Essence
is to worship Him for His sake, without fear of fire, or
hope of paradise.

Although when true worship is offered, the worshiper
is delivered from the fire, and entereth the paradise of
God's good pleasure, yet such should not be the motive
of his act. However, God's favor and grace ever flow in
accordance with the exigencies of His inscrutable
wisdom.

The most acceptable prayer is the one offered with the
utmost spirituality and radiance; its prolongation hath
not been and is not beloved by God. The more detached
and the purer the prayer, the more acceptable is it in
the presence of God.   15

Prayer, verily, bestoweth life, particularly when offered in
private and at times, such as midnight, when freed from
daily cares.   16

At the dawn of every day he [the true seeker] should commune with God and, with all his soul, persevere in the quest of his Beloved. 17

Learning the Language of Prayer

IT behooveth the servant to pray to and seek assistance from God, and to supplicate and implore His aid. Such becometh the rank of servitude, and the Lord will decree whatsoever He desireth, in accordance with His consummate wisdom. 18

Beseech thou from God's infinite grace whatsoever thou desirest. But wert thou to heed my advice, thou wouldst desire naught save entrance into the Abhá Kingdom,* and seek naught save the bounties of the beauty of the All-Glorious, may my life be sacrificed for His loved ones. This is my exhortation to thee. 19

When the sinner findeth himself wholly detached and freed from all save God, he should beg forgiveness and pardon from Him. Confession of sins and transgressions before human beings is not permissible, as it hath never been nor will ever be conducive to divine forgiveness. Moreover, such confession before people results in one's humiliation and abasement, and God—exalted be His glory—wisheth not the humiliation of His servants. Verily, He is the Compassionate, the Merciful. The sinner should, between himself and God, implore mercy from the Ocean of mercy, beg forgiveness from the Heaven of generosity. 20

Pray to God that He may strengthen you in divine virtue, so that you may be as angels in the world, and

---

*The kingdom of God. *Abhá* means "Most Glorious."

beacons of light to disclose the mysteries of the kingdom
to those with understanding hearts.   21

I entreat Thee to enable me to cleave steadfastly to Thy
love and Thy remembrance. This is, verily, within my
power, and Thou art the One that knoweth all that is in
me. Thou, in truth, art knowing, apprised of all. Deprive
me not, O my Lord, of the splendors of the light of Thy
face, whose brightness hath illuminated the whole
world. No God is there beside Thee, the Most Powerful,
the All-Glorious, the Ever-Forgiving.   22

O Thou the Compassionate God. Bestow upon me a
heart which, like unto a glass, may be illumined with the
light of Thy love, and confer upon me thoughts which
may change this world into a rose garden through the
outpourings of heavenly grace.

   Thou art the Compassionate, the Merciful. Thou art
the Great Beneficent God.   23

Praying for Others

SUPPLICATION and prayer on behalf of others will
   surely be effective.   24

It is seemly that the servant should, after each prayer,
supplicate God to bestow mercy and forgiveness upon his
parents. Thereupon God's call will be raised: "Thousand
upon thousand of what thou hast asked for thy parents
shall be thy recompense!" Blessed is he who remembereth
his parents when communing with God. There is, verily,
no God but Him, the Mighty, the Well-Beloved.   25

Pray thou that the ill-natured become good-natured and
the weak become strong.   26

As the spirit of man after putting off this material form
has an everlasting life, certainly any existing being is

capable of making progress; therefore, it is permitted to ask for advancement, forgiveness, mercy, beneficence and blessings for a man after his death because existence is capable of progression. That is why in the prayers of Bahá'u'lláh forgiveness and remission of sins are asked for those who have died. Moreover, as people in this world are in need of God, they will also need Him in the other world. The creatures are always in need, and God is absolutely independent, whether in this world or in the world to come.

The wealth of the other world is nearness to God. Consequently, it is certain that those who are near the divine court are allowed to intercede, and this intercession is approved by God. But intercession in the other world is not like intercession in this world. It is another thing, another reality, which cannot be expressed in words.   27

Answers to Prayer

GOD will answer the prayer of every servant if that prayer is urgent. His mercy is vast, illimitable. He answers the prayers of all His servants. . . .

But we ask for things which the divine wisdom does not desire for us, and there is no answer to our prayer. His wisdom does not sanction what we wish. We pray, "O God! Make me wealthy!" If this prayer were universally answered, human affairs would be at a standstill. There would be none left to work in the streets, none to till the soil, none to build, none to run the trains. Therefore, it is evident that it would not be well for us if all prayers were answered. The affairs of the world would be interfered with, energies crippled and progress hindered. But whatever we ask for which is in accord with divine wisdom, God will answer. Assuredly!

For instance, a very feeble patient may ask the doctor to give him food which would be positively dangerous to his life and condition. He may beg for roast meat. The doctor is kind and wise. He knows it would be dangerous to his patient so he refuses to allow it. The doctor is merciful; the patient, ignorant. Through the doctor's kindness the patient recovers; his life is saved. Yet the patient may cry out that the doctor is unkind, not good, because he refuses to answer his pleading.

God is merciful. In His mercy He answers the prayers of all His servants when according to His supreme wisdom it is necessary.   28

Praying with Gratitude and Thanksgiving

BE thou happy and well pleased and arise to offer thanks to God, in order that thanksgiving may conduce to the increase of bounty.   29

Thank thou the kind Father that the entire creation was adorned with the light of His Manifestation* and the heart of the contingent world found comfort in His mercy. . . .   30

Wherefore, be thankful to God for having strengthened thee to aid His Cause, for having made the flowers of knowledge and understanding to spring forth in the garden of thine heart. Thus hath His grace encompassed thee, and encompassed the whole of creation. Beware, lest thou allow anything whatsoever to grieve thee.   31

Do you realize how much you should thank God for His blessings? If you should thank Him a thousand times with each breath, it would not be sufficient because God has created and trained you. He has protected you from every affliction and prepared every gift and bestowal. Consider what a kind Father He is. He bestows His gift

---

*The divine Messenger of God through Whom God's perfections and attributes are expressed.

before you ask. We were not in the world of existence,
but as soon as we were born, we found everything
prepared for our needs and comfort without question on
our part. He has given us a kind father and compassionate
mother, provided for us two springs of salubrious milk,
pure atmosphere, refreshing water, gentle breezes and
the sun shining above our heads. In brief, He has
supplied all the necessities of life although we did not
ask for any of these great gifts. . . . He has created us in
this radiant century, a century longed for and expected by
all the sanctified souls in past periods. It is a blessed
century; it is a blessed day. The philosophers of history
have agreed that this century is equal to one hundred
past centuries. This is true from every standpoint. This is
the century of science, inventions, discoveries and
universal laws. This is the century of the revelation of
the mysteries of God. This is the century of the
effulgence of the rays of the Sun of Truth. Therefore,
you must render thanks and glorification to God that you
were born in this age. Furthermore, you have listened
to the call of Bahá'u'lláh. . . . You were asleep; you
are awakened. Your ears are attentive; your hearts are
informed. You have acquired the love of God. You have
attained to the knowledge of God. This is the most great
bestowal of God. This is the breath of the Holy Spirit.
. . . You must appreciate the value of this bounty and
engage your time in mentioning and thanking the True
One. You must live in the utmost happiness. If any
trouble or vicissitude comes into your lives, if your heart
is depressed on account of health, livelihood or vocation,
let not these things affect you. They should not cause
unhappiness, for Bahá'u'lláh has brought you divine
happiness. He has prepared heavenly food for you; He
has destined eternal bounty for you; He has bestowed
everlasting glory upon you. Therefore, these glad tidings
should cause you to soar in the atmosphere of joy forever
and ever. Render continual thanks unto God so that the
confirmations of God may encircle you all.   32

Thankfulness is of various kinds. There is a verbal
thanksgiving which is confined to a mere utterance of
gratitude. This is of no importance because perchance
the tongue may give thanks while the heart is unaware of
it. Many who offer thanks to God are of this type, their
spirits and hearts unconscious of thanksgiving. This is
mere usage, just as when we meet, receive a gift and say
thank you, speaking the words without significance. One
may say thank you a thousand times while the heart
remains thankless, ungrateful. Therefore, mere verbal
thanksgiving is without effect. But real thankfulness is a
cordial giving of thanks from the heart. When man in
response to the favors of God manifests susceptibilities of
conscience, the heart is happy, the spirit is exhilarated.
These spiritual susceptibilities are ideal thanksgiving.

There is a cordial thanksgiving, too, which expresses
itself in the deeds and actions of man when his heart is
filled with gratitude. For example, God has conferred
upon man the gift of guidance, and in thankfulness for
this great gift certain deeds must emanate from him. To
express his gratitude for the favors of God man must
show forth praiseworthy actions. In response to these
bestowals he must render good deeds, be self-sacrificing,
loving the servants of God, forfeiting even life for
them, showing kindness to all the creatures. He must be
severed from the world, attracted to the Kingdom of
Abhá,* the face radiant, the tongue eloquent, the ear
attentive, striving day and night to attain the good
pleasure of God. Whatsoever he wishes to do must be in
harmony with the good pleasure of God. He must
observe and see what is the will of God and act accord-
ingly. There can be no doubt that such commendable
deeds are thankfulness for the favors of God.

Consider how grateful anyone becomes when healed
from sickness, when treated kindly by another or when a

---

*The kingdom of God. *Abhá* means "Most Glorious."

service is rendered by another, even though it may be of the least consequence. If we forget such favors, it is an evidence of ingratitude. Then it will be said a loving kindness has been done, but we are thankless, not appreciating this love and favor. Physically and spiritually we are submerged in the sea of God's favor. He has provided our foods, drink and other requirements; His favors encompass us from all directions. The sustenances provided for man are blessings. Sight, hearing and all his faculties are wonderful gifts. These blessings are innumerable; no matter how many are mentioned, they are still endless. Spiritual blessings are likewise endless— spirit, consciousness, thought, memory, perception, ideation and other endowments. By these He has guided us, and we enter His kingdom. He has opened the doors of all good before our faces. He has vouchsafed eternal glory. He has summoned us to the kingdom of heaven. He has enriched us by the bestowals of God. Every day he has proclaimed new glad tidings. Every hour fresh bounties descend.

Consider how all the people are asleep, and ye are awake. They are dead, and ye are alive through the breaths of the Holy Spirit. They are blind while ye are endowed with perceptive sight. They are deprived of the love of God, but in your hearts it exists and is glowing. Consider these bestowals and favors.

Therefore, in thanksgiving for them ye must act in accordance with the teachings of Bahá'u'lláh. . . . This is real thanksgiving, to live in accord with these utterances. This is true thankfulness and the divine bestowal. This is thanksgiving and glorification of God.   33

Praising and Glorifying God

I GIVE praise to Thee, O my God, that the fragrance of Thy loving kindness hath enraptured me, and the gentle winds of Thy mercy have inclined me in the direction of Thy bountiful favors.   34

Immeasurably glorified and exalted art Thou. How can I
make mention of Thee, O Thou the Beloved of the
entire creation; and how can I acknowledge Thy claim,
O Thou before Whom every created thing standeth
in awe. The loftiest station to which human perception
can soar and the utmost height which the minds and
souls of men can scale are but signs created through the
potency of Thy command and tokens manifested
through the power of Thy Revelation. Far be it from
Thy glory that anyone other than Thee should make
mention of Thee or should attempt to voice Thy praise.
The very essence of every reality beareth witness to its
debarment from the precincts of the court of Thy
nearness, and the quintessence of every being testifieth to
its failure to attain Thy holy Presence. Immeasurably
glorified and exalted art Thou! That which alone beseemeth Thee is the befitting mention made by Thine Own
Self, and that only which is worthy of Thee is the
anthem of praise voiced by Thine Own Essence. . . .   35

Every time I lift up mine eyes unto Thy heaven, I call to
mind Thy highness and Thy loftiness, and Thine incomparable glory and greatness; and every time I turn my
gaze to Thine earth, I am made to recognize the
evidences of Thy power and the tokens of Thy bounty.
And when I behold the sea, I find that it speaketh to me
of Thy majesty, and of the potency of Thy might, and of
Thy sovereignty and Thy grandeur. And at whatever
time I contemplate the mountains, I am led to discover
the ensigns of Thy victory and the standards of Thine
omnipotence.   36

Glory be to Thee, O my God! The power of Thy might
beareth me witness! I can have no doubt that should
the holy breaths of Thy loving kindness and the breeze
of Thy bountiful favor cease, for less than the twinkling
of an eye, to breathe over all created things, the entire
creation would perish, and all that are in heaven and on

earth would be reduced to utter nothingness. Magnified, therefore, be the marvelous evidences of Thy transcendent power! Magnified be the potency of Thine exalted might! Magnified be the majesty of Thine all-encompassing greatness, and the energizing influence of Thy will!   37

Blessed is the spot, and the house, and the place, and the city, and the heart, and the mountain, and the refuge, and the cave, and the valley, and the land, and the sea, and the island, and the meadow where mention of God hath been made, and His praise glorified.   38

Meditation and the Revealed Word of God

ONE hour's reflection is preferable to seventy years of pious worship. . . .   39

Through the faculty of meditation man attains to eternal life; through it he receives the breath of the Holy Spirit—the bestowal of the Spirit is given in reflection and meditation.

The spirit of man is itself informed and strengthened during meditation; through it affairs of which man knew nothing are unfolded before his view. Through it he receives divine inspiration; through it he receives heavenly food. . . .

This faculty of meditation frees man from the animal nature, discerns the reality of things, puts man in touch with God.

This faculty brings forth from the invisible plane the sciences and arts. Through the meditative faculty inventions are made possible, colossal undertakings are carried out; through it governments can run smoothly. Through this faculty man enters into the very kingdom of God.

Nevertheless, some thoughts are useless to man; they are like waves moving in the sea without result. But if the faculty of meditation is bathed in the inner light and characterized with divine attributes, the results will be confirmed.

The meditative faculty is akin to the mirror; if you put it before earthly objects, it will reflect them. Therefore, if the spirit of man is contemplating earthly subjects, he will be informed of these.

But if you turn the mirror of your spirits heavenwards, . . . the rays of the Sun of Reality will be reflected in your hearts, and the virtues of the kingdom will be obtained.

Therefore, let us keep this faculty rightly directed— turning it to the heavenly Sun and not to earthly objects—so that we may discover the secrets of the kingdom, and comprehend the allegories of the Bible and the mysteries of the spirit.   40

Investigate and study the Holy Scriptures word by word so that you may attain knowledge of the mysteries hidden therein. Be not satisfied with words, but seek to understand the spiritual meanings hidden in the heart of the words. . . . These are the mysteries of God. It is not the reading of the words that profits you; it is the understanding of their meanings. Therefore, pray God that you may be enabled to comprehend the mysteries of the divine Testaments. . . .

All the texts and teachings of the holy Testaments have intrinsic spiritual meanings. They are not to be taken literally. . . . May your souls be illumined by the light of the Words of God, and may you become repositories of the mysteries of God, for no comfort is greater and no happiness is sweeter than spiritual comprehension of the divine teachings.   41

Recite ye the verses of God every morning and evening. Whoso reciteth them not hath truly failed to fulfill his pledge to the Covenant of God and His Testament, and whoso in this day turneth away therefrom, hath indeed turned away from God since time immemorial. Fear ye God, O Concourse of My servants.

"Take heed lest excessive reading and too many acts of piety in the daytime and the night season make you vainglorious. Should a person recite but a single verse from the Holy Writings in a spirit of joy and radiance, this would be better for him than reciting wearily all the Scriptures of God, the Help in Peril, the Self-Subsisting. Recite ye the verses of God in such measure that ye be not overtaken with fatigue or boredom. Burden not your souls so as to cause exhaustion and weigh them down, but, rather, endeavor to lighten them, that they may soar on the wings of revealed Verses unto the dawning place of His signs. This is conducive to nearer access unto God, were ye to comprehend." 42

Were any man to ponder in his heart that which the Pen of the Most High hath revealed and to taste of its sweetness, he would, of a certainty, find himself emptied and delivered from his own desires, and utterly subservient to the Will of the Almighty. Happy is the man that hath attained so high a station, and hath not deprived himself of so bountiful a grace. 43

O maidservant of God! Chant thou the Words of God, derive joy from their meaning, and strive to transform them into actions! 44

6

Faith and Certitude

FAITH is the magnet which draws the confirmation of the Merciful One. Service is the magnet which attracteth the heavenly strength. I hope thou wilt attain both.

1

Acknowledging the Sovereignty of God

BLESSED is the man that hath acknowledged his belief in God and in His signs, and recognized that "he shall not be asked of His doings." Such a recognition hath been made by God the ornament of every belief, and its very foundation. Upon it must depend the acceptance of every goodly deed. Fasten your eyes upon it, that haply the whisperings of the rebellious may not cause you to slip.

. . . He that hath acknowledged this principle will be endowed with the most perfect constancy. . . . Such is the teaching which God bestoweth on you, a teaching that will deliver you from all manner of doubt and perplexity, and enable you to attain unto salvation in both this world and in the next. He, verily, is the Ever-Forgiving, the Most Bountiful.

2

I testify, O my God, to that whereunto Thy chosen Ones have testified, and acknowledge that which the inmates of the all-highest Paradise and those who have circled round Thy mighty Throne have acknowledged. The kingdoms of earth and heaven are Thine, O Lord of the worlds!

3

The Signs of True Faith

THE first sign of faith is love. 4

By faith is meant, first, conscious knowledge and second, the practice of good deeds. 5

The essence of faith is fewness of words and abundance of deeds; he whose words exceed his deeds, know, verily, his death is better than his life. 6

The cornerstone of the religion of God is the acquisition of the divine perfections and the sharing in His manifold bestowals. The essential purpose of faith and belief is to ennoble the inner being of man with the outpourings of grace from on high. If this be not attained, it is, indeed, deprivation itself. It is the torment of infernal fire.

Wherefore, it is incumbent upon all Bahá'ís to ponder this very delicate and vital matter in their hearts, that, unlike other religions, they may not content themselves with the noise, the clamor, the hollowness of religious doctrine. Nay, rather, they should exemplify in every aspect of their lives those attributes and virtues that are born of God and should arise to distinguish themselves by their goodly behavior. They should justify their claim to be Bahá'ís by deeds and not by name. He is a true Bahá'í who strives by day and by night to progress and advance along the path of human endeavor, whose most cherished desire is so to live and act as to enrich and illuminate the world, whose source of inspiration is the essence of divine virtue, whose aim in life is so to conduct himself as to be the cause of infinite progress. Only when he attains unto such perfect gifts can it be said of him that he is a true Bahá'í. For in this holy dispensation, the crowning glory of bygone ages and cycles, true faith is no mere acknowledgment of the

unity of God, but rather the living of a life that will
manifest all the perfections and virtues implied in such
belief. . . .   7

Just as the conception of faith hath existed from the
beginning that hath no beginning, and will endure till
the end that hath no end, in like manner will the true
believer eternally live and endure. His spirit will
everlastingly circle round the Will of God. He will last
as long as God Himself will last.   8

The Acquisition of Certitude

VERILY, I beseech the Lord of Hosts to increase thy
faith each day over that of the previous day. . . .   9

Be confident in the bounty of thy Lord.   10

Rely upon God, thy God and the Lord of thy fathers. For
the people are wandering in the paths of delusion,
bereft of discernment to see God with their own eyes, or
hear His Melody with their own ears.   11

If thou wishest the divine knowledge and recognition,
purify thy heart from all beside God, be wholly attracted
to the ideal, beloved One; search for and choose Him
and apply thyself to rational and authoritative arguments.
For arguments are a guide to the path, and by this the
heart will be turned unto the Sun of Truth. And when
the heart is turned unto the Sun, then the eye will be
opened and will recognize the Sun through the Sun
itself. Then there will be no need of arguments, for the
Sun is altogether independent, and absolute independence is in need of nothing, including proofs. Be not like
Thomas; be thou like Peter. . . .   12

Only when the lamp of search, of earnest striving, of
longing desire, of passionate devotion, of fervid love, of

rapture, and ecstasy is kindled within the seeker's heart, and the breeze of His loving kindness is wafted upon his soul, will the darkness of error be dispelled, the mists of doubts and misgivings be dissipated, and the lights of knowledge and certitude envelop his being.　　13

The first and foremost testimony establishing His truth is His own Self. Next to this testimony is His revelation. For whoso faileth to recognize either the one or the other He hath established the words He hath revealed as proof of His reality and truth. This is, verily, an evidence of His tender mercy unto men. He hath endowed every soul with the capacity to recognize the signs of God.　14

Every man hath been, and will continue to be, able of himself to appreciate the Beauty of God, the Glorified. Had he not been endowed with such a capacity, how could he be called to account for his failure? If, in the Day when all the peoples of the earth will be gathered together, any man should, whilst standing in the presence of God, . . . say: "Inasmuch as all men have erred, and none hath been found willing to turn his face to the Truth, I, too, following their example, have grievously failed to recognize the Beauty of the Eternal," such a plea will, assuredly, be rejected. For the faith of no man can be conditioned by anyone except himself.　　15

7

Detachment and Sacrifice

Seeking the Spiritual World

THE essence of detachment is for man to turn his face towards the courts of the Lord, to enter His Presence, behold His Countenance, and stand as witness before Him.   1

O Son of Utterance! Turn thy face unto Mine and renounce all save Me; for My sovereignty endureth and My dominion perisheth not. If thou seekest another than Me, yea, if thou searchest the universe forevermore, thy quest will be in vain.   2

O ye loved ones of God! Know ye that the world is even as a mirage rising over the sands, that the thirsty mistaketh for water. The wine of this world is but a vapor in the desert, its pity and compassion but toil and trouble, the repose it proffereth only weariness and sorrow. Abandon it to those who belong to it, and turn your faces unto the kingdom of your Lord, the All-Merciful, that His grace and bounty may cast their dawning splendors over you, and a heavenly table may be sent down for you, and your Lord may bless you, and shower His riches upon you to gladden your bosoms and fill your hearts with bliss, to attract your minds, and cleanse your souls, and console your eyes.   3

O Son of Earth! Wouldst thou have Me, seek none other than Me; and wouldst thou gaze upon My beauty, close thine eyes to the world and all that is therein; for My will and the will of another than Me, even as fire and water, cannot dwell together in one heart.   4

He is not to be numbered with the people of Bahá who
followeth his mundane desires, or fixeth his heart on
things of the earth. He is My true follower who, if he
come to a valley of pure gold, will pass straight through
it aloof as a cloud, and will neither turn back, nor
pause. Such a man is, assuredly, of Me. From his garment
the Concourse on high can inhale the fragrance of
sanctity.   5

Becoming Forgetful of Self

O MY Servant! Free thyself from the fetters of this
world, and loose thy soul from the prison of self.
Seize thy chance, for it will come to thee no more.   6

Freedom is not a matter of place, but of condition. I was
happy in that prison, for those days were passed in the
path of service.*
     To me prison was freedom.
     Troubles are a rest to me.
     Death is life.
     To be despised is honor.
     Therefore, was I full of happiness all through that
prison time.
     When one is released from the prison of self, that is,
indeed, freedom! For self is the greatest prison.
     When this release takes place, one can never be
imprisoned. Unless one accepts dire vicissitudes, not
with dull resignation, but with radiant acquiescence, one
cannot attain this freedom.   7

O Son of Man! If thou lovest Me, turn away from
thyself; and if thou seekest My pleasure, regard not thine

---

*'Abdu'l-Bahá was incarcerated with His Father, Bahá'u'lláh, in
the prison in Akka, Palestine.

own, that thou mayest die in Me and I may eternally
live in thee.   8

O Son of Spirit! There is no peace for thee save by
renouncing thyself and turning unto Me; for it behooveth thee to glory in My name, not in thine own; to
put thy trust in Me and not in thyself, since I desire to be
loved alone and above all that is.   9

O Quintessence of Passion! Put away all covetousness
and seek contentment; for the covetous hath ever been
deprived, and the contented hath ever been loved and
praised.   10

Detachment is as the sun; in whatsoever heart it doth
shine it quencheth the fire of covetousness and self. He
whose sight is illumined with the light of understanding
will assuredly detach himself from the world and the
vanities thereof. . . . Let not the world and its vileness
grieve you. Happy is he whom riches fill not with
vainglory, nor poverty with sorrow.   11

Avoiding Asceticism through Moderation

DISENCUMBER yourselves of all attachment to this
world and the vanities thereof. Beware that ye
approach them not, inasmuch as they prompt you
to walk after your own lusts and covetous desires, and
hinder you from entering the straight and glorious Path.
    Know ye that by "the world" is meant your unaware-
ness of Him Who is your Maker, and your absorption
in aught else but Him. The "life to come," on the other
hand, signifieth the things that give you a safe approach
to God, the All-Glorious, the Incomparable. Whatsoever
deterreth you, in this Day, from loving God is nothing
but the world. Flee it, that ye may be numbered with the
blest. Should a man wish to adorn himself with the

ornaments of the earth, to wear its apparels, or partake
of the benefits it can bestow, no harm can befall him,
if he alloweth nothing whatever to intervene between
him and God, for God hath ordained every good thing,
whether created in the heavens or in the earth, for
such of His servants as truly believe in Him. Eat ye, O
people, of the good things which God hath allowed you,
and deprive not yourselves from His wondrous bounties.
Render thanks and praise unto Him, and be of them
that are truly thankful. 12

With reference to what is meant by an individual becoming entirely forgetful of self: The intent is that
he should rise up and sacrifice himself in the true sense,
that is, he should obliterate the promptings of the human
condition, and rid himself of such characteristics as are
worthy of blame and constitute the gloomy darkness
of this life on earth—not that he should allow his
physical health to deteriorate and his body to become
infirm. 13

The Mystery of Sacrifice

TO MAKE a sacrifice is to receive a gift. . . . 14

The mystery of "ransom" or sacrifice is a most great
subject and is inexhaustible.
    Briefly it is as follows: The moth is a sacrifice to the
candle. The spring is a sacrifice to the thirsty one.
The sincere lover is a sacrifice to the loved one, and the
longing one is a sacrifice to the beloved. The point lies in
this: He must wholly forget himself. . . . He must seek
the good pleasure of the True One, desire the face of the
True One, and walk in the path of the True One. . . .
This is the first station of sacrifice.
    The second station of sacrifice is as follows: Man must
become . . . like unto the iron thrown within the

furnace of fire. The qualities of iron, such as blackness, coldness and solidity, which belong to the earth, disappear and vanish, while the characteristics of fire, such as redness, glowing and heat, which belong to the kingdom, become apparent and visible. Therefore, iron hath sacrificed its qualities and grades to the fire, acquiring the virtues of that element.   15

Man must sever himself from the influences of the world of matter, from the world of nature and its laws; for the material world is the world of corruption and death. It is the world of evil and darkness, of animalism and ferocity, bloodthirstiness, ambition and avarice, of self-worship, egotism and passion; it is the world of nature. Man must strip himself of all these imperfections, must sacrifice these tendencies which are peculiar to the outer and material world of existence.

On the other hand, man must acquire heavenly qualities and attain divine attributes. He must become the image and likeness of God. He must seek the bounty of the eternal, become the manifestor of the love of God, the light of guidance, the tree of life and the depository of the bounties of God. That is to say, man must sacrifice the qualities and attributes of the world of nature for the qualities and attributes of the world of God.   16

Nearness to God is possible through devotion to Him, through entrance into the kingdom and service to humanity; it is attained by unity with mankind and through loving kindness to all; it is dependent upon investigation of truth, acquisition of praiseworthy virtues, service in the cause of universal peace and personal sanctification. In a word, nearness to God necessitates sacrifice of self, severance and the giving up of all to Him. Nearness is likeness.   17

Until a being setteth his foot in the plane of sacrifice, he

is bereft of every favor and grace; and this plane of
sacrifice is the realm of dying to the self, that the radiance of the living God may then shine forth.   18

Know thou that when the Son of Man yielded up His
breath to God, the whole creation wept with a great
weeping. By sacrificing Himself, however, a fresh capacity was infused into all created things. Its evidences, as
witnessed in all the peoples of the earth, are now manifest before thee. The deepest wisdom which the sages
have uttered, the profoundest learning which any mind
hath unfolded, the arts which the ablest hands have
produced, the influence exerted by the most potent of
rulers are but manifestations of the quickening power
released by His transcendent, His all-pervasive, and
resplendent Spirit.   19

Achieving Spiritual Victory

BE NOT content with the ease of a passing day, and
deprive not thyself of everlasting rest. Barter
not the garden of eternal delight for the dust-heap of a
mortal world. Up from thy prison ascend unto the
glorious meads above, and from thy mortal cage wing
thy flight unto the paradise of the Placeless.   20

"Victory" neither hath been nor will be opposition to
anyone, nor strife with any person; but, rather, what
is well pleasing is that the cities of [men's] hearts, which
are under the dominion of the hosts of selfishness and
lust, should be subdued by the sword of the Word,
of Wisdom, and of Exhortation. Everyone, then, who
desireth "victory" must first subdue the city of his own
heart with the sword of spiritual truth and of the Word,
and must protect it from remembering aught beside
God: Afterwards let him turn his regards towards the
cities of [others'] hearts. This is what is intended by
"victory." . . .   21

That seeker must at all times put his trust in God, must renounce the peoples of the earth, detach himself from the world of dust, and cleave unto Him Who is the Lord of Lords. . . . He should be content with little, and be freed from all inordinate desire. He should treasure the companionship of those that have renounced the world, and regard avoidance of boastful and worldly people a precious benefit. . . . He should consume every wayward thought with the flame of His loving mention, and, with the swiftness of lightning, pass by all else save Him. . . . He should not hesitate to offer up his life for his Beloved, nor allow the censure of the people to turn him away from the Truth.   22

Prayer for Detachment

O GOD, my God! Fill up for me the cup of detachment from all things, and in the assembly of Thy splendors and bestowals, rejoice me with the wine of loving Thee. Free me from the assaults of passion and desire, break off from me the shackles of this nether world, draw me with rapture unto Thy supernal realm, and refresh me amongst the handmaids with the breathings of Thy holiness.

O Lord, brighten Thou my face with the lights of Thy bestowals, light Thou mine eyes with beholding the signs of Thine all-subduing might; delight my heart with the glory of Thy knowledge that encompasseth all things, gladden Thou my soul with Thy soul-reviving tidings of great joy, O Thou King of this world and the kingdom above, O Thou Lord of dominion and might, that I may spread abroad Thy signs and tokens, and proclaim Thy Cause, and promote Thy Teachings, and serve Thy Law and exalt Thy Word.

Thou art, verily, the Powerful, the Ever-Giving, the Able, the Omnipotent.   23

8

Rectitude and Purity

IN BRIEF, let each one of you be as a lamp shining forth with the light of the virtues of the world of humanity. Be trustworthy, sincere, affectionate and replete with chastity. Be illumined, be spiritual, be divine, be glorious, be quickened of God, be a Bahá'í.   1

Deeds and Words

LET deeds, not words, be your adorning.   2

A man who does great good, and talks not of it, is on the way to perfection.
The man who has accomplished a small good and magnifies it in his speech is worth very little.   3

O Son of My Handmaid! Guidance hath ever been given by words, and now it is given by deeds. Everyone must show forth deeds that are pure and holy, for words are the property of all alike, whereas such deeds as these belong only to Our loved ones. Strive then with heart and soul to distinguish yourselves by your deeds. In this wise We counsel you in this holy and resplendent tablet.   4

The companions of God are, in this day, the lump that must leaven the peoples of the world. They must show forth such trustworthiness, such truthfulness and perseverance, such deeds and character that all mankind may profit by their example.   5

Beware, O people of Bahá, lest ye walk in the ways of them whose words differ from their deeds. Strive that ye may be enabled to manifest to the peoples of the earth the signs of God, and to mirror forth His commandments. Let your acts be a guide unto all mankind, for the professions of most men, be they high or low, differ from their conduct. It is through your deeds that ye can distinguish yourselves from others. 6

O army of God! Through the protection and help vouchsafed by the Blessed Beauty—may my life be a sacrifice to His loved ones—ye must conduct yourselves in such a manner that ye may stand out distinguished and brilliant as the sun among other souls. Should any one of you enter a city, he should become a center of attraction by reason of his sincerity, his faithfulness and love, his honesty and fidelity, his truthfulness and loving kindness towards all the peoples of the world, so that the people of that city may cry out and say: "This man is unquestionably a Bahá'í, for his manners, his behavior, his conduct, his morals, his nature, and disposition reflect the attributes of the Bahá'ís." Not until ye attain this station can ye be said to have been faithful to the Covenant and Testament of God. For He hath, through irrefutable Texts, entered into a binding Covenant with us all, requiring us to act in accordance with His sacred instructions and counsels. 7

Honesty and Trustworthiness

BEAUTIFY your tongues, O people, with truthfulness, and adorn your souls with the ornament of honesty. Beware, O people, that ye deal not treacherously with anyone. Be ye the trustees of God amongst His creatures, and the emblems of His generosity amidst His people. 8

Should anyone, God forbid, manifest one iota of dishonesty, or show laxity and negligence in carrying out his duties, or unlawfully exact money from the people, be it even a single penny, or secure private gains for himself, or seek personal benefits, such a person will surely be deprived of the blessings of the Almighty. Beware, beware, lest ye fall short of what hath been set forth in this letter. 9

Trustworthiness . . . is the door of security for all that dwell on earth and a token of glory on the part of the All-Merciful. He who partaketh thereof hath indeed partaken of the treasures of wealth and prosperity. Trustworthiness is the greatest portal leading unto the tranquillity and security of the people. In truth, the stability of every affair hath depended and doth depend upon it. All the domains of power, of grandeur and of wealth are illumined by its light. 10

Justice and Equity

O SON of Spirit! The best beloved of all things in My sight is justice; turn not away therefrom if thou desirest Me, and neglect it not that I may confide in thee. By its aid thou shalt see with thine own eyes and not through the eyes of others, and shalt know of thine own knowledge and not through the knowledge of thy neighbor. Ponder this in thy heart, how it behooveth thee to be. Verily, justice is My gift to thee and the sign of My loving kindness. Set it then before thine eyes. 11

Be vigilant, that ye may not do injustice to anyone, be it to the extent of a grain of mustard seed. Tread ye the path of justice, for this, verily, is the straight path. 12

Observe equity in your judgment, ye men of understanding heart! He that is unjust in his judgment is destitute of the characteristics that distinguish man's station. 13

Whoso cleaveth to justice can, under no circumstances, transgress the limits of moderation. 14

O ye beloved of the Lord! The kingdom of God is
founded upon equity and justice, and also upon mercy,
compassion, and kindness to every living soul. Strive ye,
then, with all your heart to treat compassionately all
humankind—except for those who have some selfish,
private motive, or some disease of the soul. Kindness
cannot be shown the tyrant, the deceiver, or the thief,
because, far from awakening them to the error of their
ways, it maketh them to continue in their perversity
as before. No matter how much kindliness ye may
expend upon the liar, he will but lie the more, for he
believeth you to be deceived, while ye understand him
but too well, and only remain silent out of your extreme
compassion.   15

The purpose of justice is the appearance of unity among
men.   16

Purity

O FRIENDS of the Pure and Omnipotent God! To be
pure and holy in all things is an attribute of the
consecrated soul and a necessary characteristic of the
unenslaved mind. The best of perfections is immaculacy
and the freeing of oneself from every defect. Once the
individual is, in every respect, cleansed and purified, then
will he become a focal center reflecting the Manifest
Light.
    First in a human being's way of life must be purity,
then freshness, cleanliness, and independence of spirit.
First must the stream bed be cleansed; then may the
sweet river waters be led into it. Chaste eyes enjoy the
beatific vision of the Lord and know what this encounter
meaneth; a pure sense inhaleth the fragrances that blow
from the rose gardens of His grace; a burnished heart
will mirror forth the comely face of truth. . . .
    My meaning is this, that in every aspect of life, purity
and holiness, cleanliness and refinement, exalt the human

condition and further the development of man's inner reality. Even in the physical realm, cleanliness will conduce to spirituality, as the Holy Writings clearly state. **17**

Blessed art thou and doubly blessed if thy feet be firm, thy heart tranquil through the fragrance of the Holy Spirit and thy secret and hidden thoughts pure before the Lord of Hosts! **18**

O Son of Being! Thy heart is My home; sanctify it for My descent. Thy spirit is My place of revelation; cleanse it for My manifestation. **19**

Purity and chastity have been, and still are, the most great ornaments for the handmaidens of God. God is My Witness! The brightness of the light of chastity sheddeth its illumination upon the worlds of the spirit. . . . **20**

Beware lest ye barter away the River that is life indeed for that which the souls of the pure-hearted detest. Become ye intoxicated with the wine of the love of God, and not with that which deadeneth your minds, O ye that adore Him! **21**

Christ has addressed the world, saying, "Except ye be converted, and become as little children, ye shall not enter into the kingdom of heaven"—that is, men must become pure in heart to know God. . . . The hearts of all children are of the utmost purity. They are mirrors upon which no dust has fallen. But this purity is on account of weakness and innocence, not on account of any strength and testing, for as this is the early period of their childhood, their hearts and minds are unsullied by the world. They cannot display any great intelligence. They have neither hypocrisy nor deceit. This is on account of the child's weakness, whereas the man be-

comes pure through his strength. Through the power of
intelligence he becomes simple; through the great
power of reason and understanding and not through the
power of weakness he becomes sincere. When he attains
to the state of perfection, he will receive these qualities;
his heart becomes purified, his spirit enlightened, his
soul is sensitized and tender—all through his great
strength. This is the difference between the perfect man
and the child. Both have the underlying qualities of
simplicity and sincerity. . . .   22

Make ye then a mighty effort, that the purity and sanctity
which, above all else, are cherished by 'Abdu'l-Bahá,
shall distinguish the people of Bahá; that in every kind
of excellence the people of God shall surpass all other
human beings; that both outwardly and inwardly they
shall prove superior to the rest; that for purity, immaculacy, refinement, and the preservation of health, they
shall be leaders in the vanguard of those who know. And
that by their freedom from enslavement, their knowledge, their self-control, they shall be first among the
pure, the free and the wise.   23

9

Obedience and Humility

Obedience to God

THE source of all glory is acceptance of whatsoever
the Lord hath bestowed and contentment with
that which God hath ordained.   1

Know ye that the embodiment of liberty and its symbol
is the animal. That which beseemeth man is submission
unto such restraints as will protect him from his own
ignorance, and guard him against the harm of the
mischief-maker. Liberty causeth man to overstep the
bounds of propriety, and to infringe on the dignity of his
station. It debaseth him to the level of extreme depravity
and wickedness.
   Regard men as a flock of sheep that need a shepherd
for their protection. . . .
   The liberty that profiteth you is to be found nowhere
except in complete servitude unto God, the Eternal
Truth. Whoso hath tasted of its sweetness will refuse to
barter it for all the dominion of earth and heaven.   2

The first duty prescribed by God for His servants is the
recognition of Him Who is the Dayspring of His
Revelation and the Fountain of His laws, Who represent-
eth the Godhead in both the kingdom of His Cause and
the world of creation. . . . It behooveth everyone who
reacheth this most sublime station, this summit of
transcendent glory, to observe every ordinance of Him
Who is the Desire of the world. These twin duties

are inseparable. Neither is acceptable without the other. Thus hath it been decreed by Him Who is the Source of divine inspiration.

They whom God hath endued with insight will readily recognize that the precepts laid down by God constitute the highest means for the maintenance of order in the world and the security of its peoples. . . . We, verily, have commanded you to refuse the dictates of your evil passions and corrupt desires, and not to transgress the bounds which the Pen of the Most High hath fixed, for these are the breath of life unto all created things.   3

O Son of Spirit! Ask not of Me that which We desire not for thee; then be content with what We have ordained for thy sake, for this is that which profiteth thee, if therewith thou dost content thyself.   4

Obedience through Fear of God

THE essence of wisdom is the fear of God, the dread of His scourge and punishment, and the apprehension of His justice and decree.   5

The fear of God hath ever been the prime factor in the education of His creatures. Well is it with them that have attained thereunto!

. . . Verily, I say: The fear of God hath ever been a sure defense and a safe stronghold for all the peoples of the world. It is the chief cause of the protection of mankind, and the supreme instrument for its preservation.   6

Schools must first train the children in the principles of religion, so that the Promise and the Threat recorded in the Books of God may prevent them from the things forbidden and adorn them with the mantle of the commandments; but this in such a measure that it may not injure the children by resulting in ignorant fanaticism and bigotry.   7

O people of God! That which traineth the world is justice, for it is upheld by two pillars, reward and punishment. These two pillars are the sources of life to the world.   8

Religion is a radiant light and an impregnable stronghold for the protection and welfare of the peoples of the world, for the fear of God impelleth man to hold fast to that which is good, and shun all evil. Should the lamp of religion be obscured, chaos and confusion will ensue, and the lights of fairness and justice, of tranquillity and peace cease to shine. Unto this will bear witness every man of true understanding.   9

In formulating the principles and laws a part hath been devoted to penalties which form an effective instrument for the security and protection of men. However, dread of the penalties maketh people desist only outwardly from committing vile and contemptible deeds, while that which guardeth and restraineth man both outwardly and inwardly hath been and still is the fear of God. It is man's true protector and his spiritual guardian. It behooveth him to cleave tenaciously unto that which will lead to the appearance of this supreme bounty.   10

Obedience through Love of God

THE Tongue of My power hath, from the heaven of My omnipotent glory, addressed to My creation these words: "Observe My commandments, for the love of My beauty."   11

The essence of love is for man to turn his heart to the Beloved One, and sever himself from all else but Him,

and desire naught save that which is the desire of his
Lord.   12

O Son of Being! Walk in My statutes for love of Me, and
deny thyself that which thou desirest if thou seekest
My pleasure.   13

Humility

IF THOU art seeking everlasting glory, choose humility in the path of the True One.   14

Humility exalteth man to the heaven of glory and power,
whilst pride abaseth him to the depths of wretchedness
and degradation.   15

O Son of Man! Humble thyself before Me, that I may
graciously visit thee. Arise for the triumph of My cause,
that while yet on earth thou mayest obtain the victory. 16

They who are the beloved of God, in whatever place
they gather and whomsoever they may meet, must
evince, in their attitude towards God, and in the manner
of their celebration of His praise and glory, such humility
and submissiveness that every atom of the dust beneath
their feet may attest the depth of their devotion. . . .
They should conduct themselves in such manner that the
earth upon which they tread may never be allowed to
address to them such words as these: "I am to be
preferred above you. For witness, how patient I am in
bearing the burden which the husbandman layeth upon
me. I am the instrument that continually imparteth unto
all beings the blessings with which He Who is the
Source of all grace hath entrusted me. Notwithstanding
the honor conferred upon me, and the unnumbered
evidences of my wealth—a wealth that supplieth the
needs of all creation—behold the measure of my humility; witness with what absolute submissiveness I allow
myself to be trodden beneath the feet of men. . . ."   17

Every man of discernment, while walking upon the earth, feeleth indeed abashed, inasmuch as he is fully aware that the thing which is the source of his prosperity, his wealth, his might, his exaltation, his advancement and power is, as ordained by God, the very earth which is trodden beneath the feet of all men. There can be no doubt that whoever is cognizant of this truth is cleansed and sanctified from all pride, arrogance, and vainglory. 18

O army of God! Whensoever ye behold a person whose entire attention is directed toward the Cause of God; whose only aim is this, to make the Word of God to take effect; who, day and night, with pure intent, is rendering service to the Cause; from whose behavior not the slightest trace of egotism or private motives is discerned—who, rather, wandereth distracted in the wilderness of the love of God, and drinketh only from the cup of the knowledge of God, and is utterly engrossed in spreading the sweet savors of God, and is enamored of the holy verses of the kingdom of God—know ye for a certainty that this individual will be supported and reinforced by heaven; that like unto the morning star, he will forever gleam brightly out of the skies of eternal grace. But if he show the slightest taint of selfish desires and self-love, his efforts will lead to nothing, and he will be destroyed and left hopeless at the last. 19

Self-love is a strange trait and the means of the destruction of many important souls in the world. If man be imbued with all good qualities but be selfish, all the other virtues will fade or pass away, and eventually he will grow worse. 20

O Children of Men! Know ye not why We created you all from the same dust? That no one should exalt himself over the other. Ponder at all times in your hearts how ye were created. Since We have created you all from one

same substance, it is incumbent on you to be even as one
soul, to walk with the same feet, eat with the same
mouth and dwell in the same land, that from your
inmost being, by your deeds and actions, the signs of
oneness and the essence of detachment may be made
manifest. Such is My counsel to you, O concourse
of light! Heed ye this counsel that ye may obtain the
fruit of holiness from the tree of wondrous glory.   21

You must manifest complete love and affection toward all
mankind. Do not exalt yourselves above others, but
consider all as your equals, recognizing them as the
servants of one God.   22

He [the seeker] must never seek to exalt himself above
anyone, must wash away from the tablet of his heart
every trace of pride and vainglory, must cling unto
patience and resignation, observe silence, and refrain
from idle talk.   23

If ye meet the abased or the downtrodden, turn not away
disdainfully from them, for the King of Glory ever
watcheth over them and surroundeth them with such
tenderness as none can fathom except them that have
suffered their wishes and desires to be merged in the
Will of your Lord, the Gracious, the All-Wise. O ye rich
ones of the earth! Flee not from the face of the poor
that lieth in the dust; nay, rather, befriend him and suffer
him to recount the tale of the woes with which God's
inscrutable Decree hath caused him to be afflicted.
By the righteousness of God! Whilst ye consort with
him, the Concourse on high will be looking upon you,
will be interceding for you, will be extolling your names
and glorifying your action. Blessed are the learned that
pride not themselves on their attainments; and well is
it with the righteous that mock not the sinful, but,
rather, conceal their misdeeds, so that their own shortcomings may remain veiled to men's eyes.   24

In accordance with the divine teachings in this glorious
dispensation we should not belittle anyone and call
him ignorant, saying, "You know not, but I know."
Rather, we should look upon others with respect, and
when attempting to explain and demonstrate, we should
speak as if we are investigating the truth, saying, "Here
these things are before us. Let us investigate to determine
where and in what form the truth can be found." The
teacher should not consider himself as learned and others
ignorant. Such a thought breedeth pride, and pride is
not conducive to influence. The teacher should not see in
himself any superiority; he should speak with the
utmost kindliness, lowliness and humility, for such
speech exerteth influence and educateth the souls.   25

Show forbearance and benevolence and love to one
another. Should anyone among you be incapable of
grasping a certain truth, or be striving to comprehend it,
show forth, when conversing with him, a spirit of
extreme kindliness and goodwill. Help him to see and
recognize the truth, without esteeming yourself to be, in
the least, superior to him, or to be possessed of greater
endowments.

The whole duty of man in this day is to attain that
share of the flood of grace which God poureth forth for
him. Let none, therefore, consider the largeness or
smallness of the receptacle. The portion of some might
lie in the palm of a man's hand, the portion of others
might fill a cup, and of others even a gallon measure.   26

Prayers for Humility and Obedience

I BESEECH Thee, O Thou Who art the Lord of all
names, by Thy name through which Thou hast
subdued all created things, to graciously aid Thy servants
and Thy loved ones . . . to fix their gaze at all times
upon Thy pleasure, and to yield Thee thanks for the
evidences of Thine irrevocable decree. For Thou art,

verily, praiseworthy in all that Thou hast done in the
past, or wilt do in the future, and art to be obeyed
in whatsoever Thou hast wished or wilt wish, and to be
loved in all that Thou hast desired or wilt desire. Thou
lookest upon them that are dear to Thee with the eyes of
Thy loving kindness, and sendest down for them only
that which will profit them through Thy grace and Thy
gifts.   27

I implore Thee, O my Lord, by Thy name the splendors
of which have encompassed the earth and the heavens,
to enable me so to surrender my will to what Thou hast
decreed in Thy Tablets, that I may cease to discover
within me any desire except what Thou didst desire
through the power of Thy sovereignty, and any will save
what Thou didst destine for me by Thy will.   28

Thine is the command at all times, O Thou Who art the
Lord of all names; and mine is resignation and willing
submission to Thy will, O Creator of the heavens!   29

10

Tests and Ordeals

The Benefits of Tests

THOU hast asked about ordeals, adversities and tribulations, whether they are of God or the result of man's evil deeds.

Know thou that ordeals are of two kinds: One is for tests, and the other for punishment of misdeeds. That which is for testing is for one's education and development, and that which is for punishment of deeds is severe retribution.

The father and the teacher sometimes show tenderness towards the children and at other times deal harshly with them. Such severity is for educational purposes; it is true tenderness and absolute bounty and grace. Although in appearance it is wrath, in reality it is kindness. Although outwardly it is an ordeal, inwardly it is a cooling draught.

In both cases prayers and supplications should be offered at the sacred Threshold, so that thou mayest remain firm in tests, and patient in ordeals. 1

O Son of Man! If adversity befall thee not in My path, how canst thou walk in the ways of them that are content with My pleasure? If trials afflict thee not in thy longing to meet Me, how wilt thou attain the light in thy love for My beauty? 2

Tests are benefits from God, for which we should thank Him. Grief and sorrow do not come to us by chance; they are sent to us by the divine mercy for our own perfecting.

While a man is happy, he may forget his God; but when grief comes and sorrows overwhelm him, then will he remember his Father who is in Heaven, and who is able to deliver him from his humiliations.

Men who suffer not, attain no perfection. The plant most pruned by the gardeners is that one which, when the summer comes, will have the most beautiful blossoms and the most abundant fruit.

The laborer cuts up the earth with his plough, and from that earth comes the rich and plentiful harvest. The more a man is chastened, the greater is the harvest of spiritual virtues shown forth by him. A soldier is no good general until he has been in the front of the fiercest battle and has received the deepest wounds. 3

The mind and spirit of man advance when he is tried by suffering. The more the ground is ploughed, the better the seed will grow, the better the harvest will be. Just as the plough furrows the earth deeply, purifying it of weeds and thistles, so suffering and tribulation free man from the petty affairs of this worldly life until he arrives at a state of complete detachment. His attitude in this world will be that of divine happiness. Man is, so to speak, unripe: The heat of the fire of suffering will mature him. Look back to the times past, and you will find that the greatest men have suffered most. 4

I know of a certainty, by virtue of my love for Thee, that Thou wilt never cause tribulations to befall any soul unless Thou desirest to exalt his station in Thy celestial Paradise and to buttress his heart in this earthly life with the bulwark of Thine all-compelling power, that it may not become inclined toward the vanities of this world. 5

The Meaning of Tests

AS TO tests, these are inevitable. Hast thou not heard and read how there appeared trials from God in the

days of Jesus, and thereafter, and how the winds of tests
became severe? Even the glorious Peter was not relieved
from the claws of trials. He wavered, then he repented
and mourned the mourning of a bereaved one, and
his lamentations reached the realms on high. Is it, then,
possible to be saved from the trials of God? Nay, by
the righteousness of the Lord! There is a great wisdom
therein of which no one is aware save the wise and
knowing.

Were it not for tests, pure gold could not be distinguished from the impure. Were it not for tests, the
courageous could not be separated from the cowardly.
Were it not for tests, the people of faithfulness could not
be known from the disloyal. Were it not for tests, the
intellectuals and the faculties of the scholars in great
colleges would not develop. Were it not for tests, spar-
kling gems could not be known from worthless pebbles.
Were it not for tests, nothing would progress in this
contingent world. Were it not for tests, the Fishermen
could not be distinguished from Annas and Caiaphas,
who occupied positions of honor and value.

Were it not for tests, the face of Mary, the Magdalene,
would not shed its light of steadfastness and certitude
upon all horizons. These are some insights into the
wisdom of tests which we have unfolded unto thee that
thou mayest become cognizant of the mysteries of
God in every cycle. Verily, I pray God to illumine your
faces as pure gold in the fire of tests.   6

I ask of God that thou, His husbandman, shalt plough
the hard and stony ground, and water it, and scatter seeds
therein—for this will show how skillful is the farmer,
while any man can sow and till where the ground is soft,
and clear of brambles and thorns.   7

To attain eternal happiness one must suffer. He who has
reached the state of self-sacrifice has true joy. Temporal
joy will vanish.   8

The souls who bear the tests of God become the manifestations of great bounties; for the divine trials cause some souls to become entirely lifeless, while they cause the holy souls to ascend to the highest degree of love and steadfastness. They cause progress, just as they cause retrogression. 9

But for tribulations, how could the assured be distinguished from the doubters among Thy servants? 10

How many the leaves which the tempests of trials have caused to fall, and how many, too, are those which, clinging tenaciously to the tree of Thy Cause, have remained unshaken by the tests that have assailed them, O Thou Who art our Lord, the Most Merciful! 11

The Fruits of Tests and Afflictions

DO YE not look upon the beginning of the affairs; attach your hearts to the ends and results. The present period is like unto the sowing time. Undoubtedly, it is impregnated with perils and difficulties, but in the future many a harvest shall be gathered, and benefits and results will become apparent. When one considereth the issue and the end, exhaustless joy and happiness will dawn. 12

O My servants! Sorrow not if, in these days and on this earthly plane, things contrary to your wishes have been ordained and manifested by God, for days of blissful joy, of heavenly delight, are assuredly in store for you. Worlds, holy and spiritually glorious, will be unveiled to your eyes. You are destined by Him, in this world and hereafter, to partake of their benefits, to share in their joys, and to obtain a portion of their sustaining grace. To each and every one of them you will, no doubt, attain. 13

O ye homeless and wanderers in the Path of God!

Prosperity, contentment, and freedom, however much
desired and conducive to the gladness of the human
heart, can in no wise compare with the trials of homelessness and adversity in the pathway of God; for such
exile and banishment are blessed by the divine favor, and
are surely followed by the mercy of Providence. The
joy of tranquillity in one's home, and the sweetness of
freedom from all cares shall pass away, whilst the blessing
of homelessness shall endure forever, and its far-reaching
results shall be made manifest.   14

As to the subject of babes and children and weak ones
who are afflicted by the hands of the oppressors . . . for
those souls there is a recompense in another world . . .
that suffering is the greatest mercy of God. Verily,
that mercy of the Lord is far better than all the comfort
of this world and the growth and development apper-
taining to this place of mortality.   15

Learning to Accept Tests

BE generous in prosperity, and thankful in adversity. 16

Be thou neither grieved nor despondent over what hath
come to pass. This trouble overtook thee as thou didst
walk the path of God; wherefore it should bring
thee joy.   17

If anyone revile you, or trouble touch you, in the path of
God, be patient, and put your trust in Him Who heareth,
Who seeth.   18

He will never deal unjustly with anyone; neither will He
task a soul beyond its power. He, verily, is the Compassionate, the All-Merciful.   19

O army of God! When calamity striketh, be ye patient

and composed. However afflictive your sufferings may be, stay ye undisturbed, and with perfect confidence in the abounding grace of God, brave ye the tempest of tribulations and fiery ordeals. 20

Whosoever, O my Lord, is impatient in the tribulations befalling him in Thy path hath not drunk of the cup of Thy love nor tasted of the sweetness of Thy remembrance. 21

Armed with the power of Thy name, nothing can ever hurt me, and with Thy love in my heart all the world's afflictions can in no wise alarm me. 22

Let nothing grieve thee, and be thou angered at none. It behooveth thee to be content with the Will of God, and a true and loving and trusted friend to all the peoples of the earth, without any exceptions whatever. This is the quality of the sincere, the way of the saints, the emblem of those who believe in the unity of God, and the raiment of the people of Bahá. 23

O God! Refresh and gladden my spirit. Purify my heart. Illumine my powers. I lay all my affairs in Thy hand. Thou art my Guide and my Refuge. I will no longer be sorrowful and grieved; I will be a happy and joyful being. O God! I will no longer be full of anxiety, nor will I let trouble harass me. I will not dwell on the unpleasant things of life.
    O God! Thou art more friend to me than I am to myself. I dedicate myself to Thee, O Lord. 24

Relying on God

BE NOT grieved if thy circumstances become exacting, and problems press upon thee from all sides. Verily, thy Lord changeth grief into joy, hardship into comfort, and affliction into absolute ease. 25

O God! Recompense those who endure patiently in Thy
days and strengthen their hearts to walk undeviatingly
in the path of Truth. Grant then, O Lord, such goodly
gifts as would enable them to gain admittance into Thy
blissful Paradise.   26

Aware as I am, O my God, that Thou wilt send down
upon Thy servants only what is good for them, I nevertheless beseech Thee, by Thy name which overshadow-
eth all things, to raise up, for their assistance and as a
sign of Thy grace and as an evidence of Thy power,
those who will keep them safe from all their adversaries.
    Potent art Thou to do Thy pleasure. Thou art, verily,
the Supreme Ruler, the Almighty, the Help in Peril,
the Self-Subsisting.   27

Prayers for Assistance and Protection

IS THERE any Remover of difficulties save God? Say:
    Praised be God! He is God! All are His servants,
and all abide by His bidding!   28

I adjure Thee by Thy might, O my God! Let no harm
beset me in times of tests, and in moments of heedlessness guide my steps aright through Thine inspiration.
Thou art God; potent art Thou to do what Thou
desirest. No one can withstand Thy Will or thwart Thy
Purpose.   29

O my Lord! Thou knowest that the people are encircled
with pain and calamities and are environed with hardships and trouble. Every trial doth attack man, and every
dire adversity doth assail him like unto the assault of a
serpent. There is no shelter and asylum for him except
under the wing of Thy protection, preservation, guard
and custody.
    O Thou the Merciful One! O my Lord! Make Thy
protection my armor, Thy preservation my shield,

humbleness before the door of Thy oneness my guard, and Thy custody and defense my fortress and my abode. Preserve me from the suggestions of self and desire, and guard me from every sickness, trial, difficulty and ordeal.

Verily, Thou art the Protector, the Guardian, the Preserver, the Sufficer, and, verily, Thou art the Merciful of the Most Merciful. 30

Say: God sufficeth unto me; He is the One Who holdeth in His grasp the kingdom of all things. Through the power of His hosts of heaven and earth and whatever lieth between them, He protecteth whomsoever among His servants He willeth. God, in truth, keepeth watch over all things.

Immeasurably exalted art Thou, O Lord! Protect us from what lieth in front of us and behind us, above our heads, on our right, on our left, below our feet and every other side to which we are exposed. Verily, Thy protection over all things is unfailing. 31

11

Practical Applications of the Spiritual Life

Service to Humanity

BE YE loving fathers to the orphan, and a refuge to the helpless, and a treasury for the poor, and a cure for the ailing. Be ye the helpers of every victim of oppression, the patrons of the disadvantaged. Think ye at all times of rendering some service to every member of the human race. 1

There is no greater result than bonds of service in the divine kingdom and attainment to the good pleasure of the Lord. Therefore, I desire that your hearts may be directed to the kingdom of God, that your intentions may be pure and sincere, your purposes turned toward altruistic accomplishment unmindful of your own welfare; nay, rather, may all your intentions center in the welfare of humanity, and may you seek to sacrifice yourselves in the pathway of devotion to mankind. Even as Jesus Christ forfeited His life, may you, likewise, offer yourselves in the threshold of sacrifice for the betterment of the world; and just as Bahá'u'lláh suffered severe ordeals and calamities nearly fifty years for you, may you be willing to undergo difficulties and withstand catastrophes for humanity in general. 2

Ye must in this matter—that is, the serving of human-kind—lay down your very lives, and as ye yield your-selves, rejoice. 3

Service to humanity is service to God. 4

O son of man! If thine eyes be turned towards mercy, forsake the things that profit thee and cleave unto that which will profit mankind. And if thine eyes be turned towards justice, choose thou for thy neighbor that which thou choosest for thyself.   5

How excellent, how honorable is man if he arises to fulfill his responsibilities; how wretched and contemptible, if he shuts his eyes to the welfare of society and wastes his precious life in pursuing his own selfish interests and personal advantages. Supreme happiness is man's, and he beholds the signs of God in the world and in the human soul, if he urges on the steed of high endeavor in the arena of civilization and justice.   6

You must consider all His servants as your own family and relations. Direct your whole effort toward the happiness of those who are despondent, bestow food upon the hungry, clothe the needy, and glorify the humble. Be a helper to every helpless one, and manifest kindness to your fellow creatures in order that ye may attain the good pleasure of God. This is conducive to the illumination of the world of humanity and eternal felicity for yourselves.   7

If thou seekest eternal glory, let thyself be humble and meek in the presence of the beloved of God; make thyself the servant of all, and serve all alike. The service of the friends belongeth to God, not to them. Strive to become a source of harmony, spirituality and joyfulness to the hearts of the friends. . . .   8

If thou seekest after a work which is brighter and more attractive, sweeter and more delightful than all the affairs, it is thralldom at the threshold of the Almighty and servitude to His Highness the Lord of Might.   9

Acquiring Knowledge and Education

KNOWLEDGE is one of the wondrous gifts of God. It is incumbent upon everyone to acquire it.   10

There are certain pillars which have been established as the unshakable supports of the Faith of God. The mightiest of these is learning and the use of the mind, the expansion of consciousness, and insight into the realities of the universe and the hidden mysteries of Almighty God.

To promote knowledge is thus an inescapable duty imposed on every one of the friends of God.   11

Man is the supreme Talisman. Lack of a proper education hath, however, deprived him of that which he doth inherently possess. Through a word proceeding out of the mouth of God he was called into being; by one word more he was guided to recognize the Source of his education; by yet another word his station and destiny were safeguarded. The Great Being saith: Regard man as a mine rich in gems of inestimable value. Education can, alone, cause it to reveal its treasures, and enable mankind to benefit therefrom.   12

Knowledge is as wings to man's life, and a ladder for his ascent. Its acquisition is incumbent upon everyone. The knowledge of such sciences, however, should be acquired as can profit the peoples of the earth, and not those which begin with words and end with words. Great, indeed, is the claim of scientists and craftsmen on the peoples of the world. . . . Happy are those possessed of a hearing ear. In truth, knowledge is a veritable treasure for man, and a source of glory, of bounty, of joy, of exaltation, of cheer and gladness unto him.   13

Although to acquire the sciences and arts is the greatest

glory of mankind, this is so only on condition that man's river flow into the mighty sea, and draw from God's ancient source His inspiration. When this cometh to pass, then every teacher is as a shoreless ocean, every pupil a prodigal fountain of knowledge. If, then, the pursuit of knowledge lead to the beauty of Him Who is the Object of all knowledge, how excellent that goal; but if not, a mere drop will perhaps shut a man off from flooding grace, for with learning cometh arrogance and pride, and it bringeth on error and indifference to God.

The sciences of today are bridges to reality; if then they lead not to reality, naught remains but fruitless illusion. By the one true God! If learning be not a means of access to Him, the Most Manifest, it is nothing but evident loss.   14

Work and Worship

MAN should know his own self and recognize that which leadeth unto loftiness or lowliness, glory or abasement, wealth or poverty. Having attained the stage of fulfillment and reached his maturity, man standeth in need of wealth, and such wealth as he acquireth through crafts or professions is commendable and praiseworthy in the estimation of men of wisdom. . . .   15

It is enjoined upon every one of you to engage in some form of occupation, such as crafts, trades and the like. We have graciously exalted your engagement in such work to the rank of worship unto God, the True One. Ponder ye in your hearts the grace and the blessings of God and render thanks unto Him at eventide and at dawn. Waste not your time in idleness and sloth. Occupy yourselves with that which profiteth yourselves and others. . .

The most despised of men in the sight of God are those who sit idly and beg. Hold ye fast unto the cord of

material means, placing your whole trust in God, the
Provider of all means. When anyone occupieth himself
in a craft or trade, such occupation itself is regarded
in the estimation of God as an act of worship; and this is
naught but a token of His infinite and all-pervasive
bounty.   16

Thou must endeavor greatly so that thou mayest become
unique in thy profession and famous in those parts,
because attaining perfection in one's profession in this
merciful period is considered to be worship of God. And
whilst thou art occupied with thy profession, thou
canst remember the True One.   17

In the Bahá'í Cause arts, sciences and all crafts are
[counted as] worship. The man who makes a piece of
notepaper to the best of his ability, conscientiously,
concentrating all his forces on perfecting it, is giving
praise to God. Briefly, all effort and exertion put forth by
man from the fullness of his heart is worship, if it is
prompted by the highest motives and the will to do
service to humanity. This is worship: to serve mankind
and to minister to the needs of the people. Service is
prayer.   18

Therefore, strive that your actions day by day may be
beautiful prayers. Turn towards God, and seek always to
do that which is right and noble.   19

True reliance is for the servant to pursue his profession
and calling in this world, to hold fast unto the Lord,
to seek naught but His grace, inasmuch as in His Hands
is the destiny of all His servants.   20

O My Servant! The best of men are they that earn a
livelihood by their calling and spend upon themselves
and upon their kindred for the love of God, the Lord of
all worlds.   21

Wealth and Poverty

O SON of Man! Should prosperity befall thee, rejoice not, and should abasement come upon thee, grieve not, for both shall pass away and be no more.   22

O Son of Being! If poverty overtake thee, be not sad; for in time the Lord of wealth shall visit thee. Fear not abasement, for glory shall one day rest on thee.   23

The essence of wealth is love for Me; whoso loveth Me is the possessor of all things, and he that loveth Me not is, indeed, of the poor and needy. This is that which the Finger of Glory and Splendor hath revealed.   24

O Ye That Pride Yourselves on Mortal Riches! Know ye in truth that wealth is a mighty barrier between the seeker and his desire, the lover and his beloved. The rich, but for a few, shall in no wise attain the court of His presence nor enter the city of content and resignation. Well is it then with him who, being rich, is not hindered by his riches from the eternal kingdom, nor deprived by them of imperishable dominion. By the Most Great Name! The splendor of such a wealthy man shall illuminate the dwellers of heaven even as the sun enlightens the people of the earth!   25

The essence of understanding is to testify to one's poverty, and submit to the Will of the Lord, the Sovereign, the Gracious, the All-Powerful.   26

Wealth is praiseworthy in the highest degree, if it is acquired by an individual's own efforts and the grace of God, in commerce, agriculture, art and industry, and if it be expended for philanthropic purposes. Above all, if a judicious and resourceful individual should initiate measures which would universally enrich the masses of the people, there could be no undertaking greater

than this, and it would rank in the sight of God as the
supreme achievement, for such a benefactor would
supply the needs and insure the comfort and well-being
of a great multitude. Wealth is most commendable,
provided the entire population is wealthy. If, however, a
few have inordinate riches while the rest are impover-
ished, and no fruit or benefit accrues from that wealth,
then it is only a liability to its possessor. If, on the other
hand, it is expended for the promotion of knowledge,
the founding of elementary and other schools, the
encouragement of art and industry, the training of orphans and the poor—in brief, if it is dedicated to the
welfare of society—its possessor will stand out before
God and man as the most excellent of all who live
on earth and will be accounted as one of the people of
paradise.   27

O Ye Rich Ones on Earth! The poor in your midst are
My trust; guard ye My trust, and be not intent only
on your own ease.   28

Those souls who are of the kingdom eagerly wish to be
of service to the poor, to sympathize with them, to show
kindness to the miserable and to make their lives
fruitful. Happy art thou that thou hast such a wish.   29

They who are possessed of riches . . . must have the
utmost regard for the poor, for great is the honor destined by God for those poor who are steadfast in
patience. By My life! There is no honor, except what
God may please to bestow, that can compare to this
honor. Great is the blessedness awaiting the poor that
endure patiently and conceal their sufferings, and well is
it with the rich who bestow their riches on the needy
and prefer them before themselves.
  Please God, the poor may exert themselves and strive
to earn the means of livelihood. This is a duty which,
in this most great Revelation, hath been prescribed unto

everyone, and is accounted in the sight of God as a
goodly deed. Whoso observeth this duty, the help of the
invisible One shall most certainly aid him. He can
enrich, through His grace, whomsoever He pleaseth. He,
verily, hath power over all things. . . .   30

Generosity and Sharing

O SON of Man! Bestow My wealth upon My poor,
that in heaven thou mayest draw from stores of
unfading splendor and treasures of imperishable glory. 31

[The true seeker] should succor the dispossessed, and
never withhold his favor from the destitute. He should
show kindness to animals, how much more unto his
fellowman, to him who is endowed with the power of
utterance.   32

Among the teachings of Bahá'u'lláh is voluntary sharing
of one's property with others among mankind. This
voluntary sharing is greater than equality, and consists in
this, that man should not prefer himself to others, but,
rather, should sacrifice his life and property for others.
But this should not be introduced by coercion so that it
becomes a law and man is compelled to follow it. Nay,
rather, man should voluntarily and of his own choice
sacrifice his property and life for others, and spend
willingly for the poor. . . .   33

Man reacheth perfection through good deeds, voluntarily
performed, not through good deeds the doing of which
was forced upon him. And sharing is a personally chosen
righteous act: That is, the rich should extend assistance
to the poor; they should expend their substance for
the poor, but of their own free will, and not because the
poor have gained this end by force. For the harvest of
force is turmoil and the ruin of the social order. On the
other hand, voluntary sharing, the freely chosen expend-

ing of one's substance, leadeth to society's comfort and
peace. It lighteth up the world; it bestoweth honor upon
humankind.   **34**

Charity is pleasing and praiseworthy in the sight of God
and is regarded as a prince among goodly deeds. . . .
Blessed is he who preferreth his brother before himself. **35**

Speech and Courtesy

O PEOPLE of God! I admonish you to observe
courtesy, for above all else it is the prince of virtues. Well is it with him who is illumined with the light
of courtesy and is attired with the vesture of uprightness.
Whoso is endued with courtesy hath indeed attained a
sublime station.   **36**

Never speak disparagingly of others, but praise without
distinction. Pollute not your tongues by speaking evil
of another.   **37**

[A true] seeker should also regard backbiting as grievous
error, and keep himself aloof from its dominion, inasmuch as backbiting quencheth the light of the heart, and
extinguisheth the life of the soul.   **38**

The tongue is a smoldering fire, and excess of speech a
deadly poison. Material fire consumeth the body, whereas
the fire of the tongue devoureth both heart and soul.
The force of the former lasteth but for a time, whilst the
effects of the latter endure a century.   **39**

O Son of Being! Ascribe not to any soul that which thou
wouldst not have ascribed to thee, and say not that
which thou doest not. This is My command unto thee,
do thou observe it.   **40**

12

Health and Healing

JOY gives us wings! In times of joy our strength is more vital, our intellect keener. . . . But when sadness visits us, we become weak; our strength leaves us. . . . 1

Although ill health is one of the unavoidable conditions of man, truly it is hard to bear. The bounty of good health is the greatest of all gifts. 2

If the health and well-being of the body be expended in the path of the kingdom, this is very acceptable and praiseworthy; and if it be expended to the benefit of the human world in general— even though it be to their material benefit—and be a means of doing good, that is also acceptable. But if the health and welfare of man be spent in sensual desires, in a life on the animal plane, and in devilish pursuits—then disease were better than such health; nay, death itself were preferable to such a life. If thou art desirous of health, wish thou health for serving the kingdom. I hope that thou mayest attain perfect insight, inflexible resolution, complete health, and spiritual and physical strength in order that thou mayest drink from the fountain of eternal life and be assisted by the spirit of divine confirmation. 3

Causes of Illness

THE provoking cause of disease—that is to say, the cause of the entrance of disease into the human body—is either a physical one or is the effect of excitement of the nerves.

But the principal causes of disease are physical, for the human body is composed of numerous elements, but in the measure of an especial equilibrium. As long as this equilibrium is maintained, man is preserved from disease; but if this essential balance, which is the pivot of the constitution, is disturbed, the constitution is disordered, and disease will supervene.

. . . When by remedies and treatments the equilibrium is reestablished, the disease is banished. . . . So long as the aim is the readjustment of the constituents of the body, it can be effected either by medicine or by food.

The majority of the diseases which overtake man also overtake the animal, but the animal is not cured by drugs. In the mountains, as in the wilderness, the animal's physician is the power of taste and smell. The sick animal smells the plants that grow in the wilderness; he eats those that are sweet and fragrant to his smell and taste, and is cured. . . .

It is, therefore, evident that it is possible to cure by foods, aliments and fruits; but as today the science of medicine is imperfect, this fact is not yet fully grasped. When the science of medicine reaches perfection, treatment will be given by foods, aliments, fragrant fruits and vegetables, and by various waters, hot and cold in temperature.   4

It is certainly the case that sins are a potent cause of physical ailments. If humankind were free from the defilements of sin and waywardness, and lived according to a natural, inborn equilibrium, without following wherever their passions led, it is undeniable that diseases would no longer take the ascendant, nor diversify with such intensity.

But man hath perversely continued to serve his lustful appetites, and he would not content himself with simple foods. Rather, he prepared for himself food that was compounded of many ingredients, of substances differing one from the other. With this, and with the perpetrating

of vile and ignoble acts, his attention was engrossed,
and he abandoned the temperance and moderation of a
natural way of life. The result was the engendering
of diseases both violent and diverse.

For the animal, as to its body, is made up of the same
constituent elements as man. Since, however, the animal
contenteth itself with simple foods and striveth not to
indulge its importunate urges to any great degree,
and committeth no sins, its ailments relative to man's are
few. We see clearly, therefore, how powerful are sin and
contumacy as pathogenic factors. And once engendered,
these diseases become compounded, multiply, and are
transmitted to others. Such are the spiritual, inner causes
of sickness.

The outer, physical causal factor in disease, however, is
a disturbance in the balance, the proportionate equilibrium of all those elements of which the human body is
composed. To illustrate: The body of man is a compound
of many constituent substances, each component being
present in a prescribed amount, contributing to the
essential equilibrium of the whole. So long as these constituents remain in their due proportion, according to the
natural balance of the whole—that is, no component
suffereth a change in its natural proportionate degree and
balance, no component being either augmented or
decreased—there will be no physical cause for the incursion of disease.

For example, the starch component must be present to
a given amount, and the sugar to a given amount. So
long as each remaineth in its natural proportion to the
whole, there will be no cause for the onset of disease.
When, however, these constituents vary as to their
natural and due amounts—that is, when they are augmented or diminished—it is certain that this will provide
for the inroads of disease. . . .

This question requireth the most careful investigation.
When highly skilled physicians shall fully examine this

matter, thoroughly and perseveringly, it will be clearly
seen that the incursion of disease is due to a disturbance
in the relative amounts of the body's component substances, and that treatment consisteth in adjusting these
relative amounts, and that this can be apprehended
and made possible by means of foods.   5

Various Methods of Healing

THERE are two ways of healing sickness, material
means and spiritual means. The first is by the treatment of physicians; the second consisteth in prayers
offered by the spiritual ones to God and in turning to
Him. Both means should be used and practiced.

Illnesses which occur by reason of physical causes
should be treated by doctors with medical remedies;
those which are due to spiritual causes disappear through
spiritual means. Thus an illness caused by affliction,
fear, nervous impressions, will be healed more effectively
by spiritual rather than by physical treatment. Hence
both kinds of treatment should be followed; they are not
contradictory. Therefore, thou shouldst also accept
physical remedies inasmuch as these, too, have come
from the mercy and favor of God, Who hath revealed
and made manifest medical science so that His servants
may profit from this kind of treatment also. Thou
shouldst give equal attention to spiritual treatments, for
they produce marvelous effects.

Now, if thou wishest to know the true remedy which
will heal man from all sickness and will give him the
health of the divine kingdom, know that it is the
precepts and teachings of God. Focus thine attention
upon them.   6

The science of medicine is still in a condition of infancy;
it has not reached maturity. But when it has reached
this point, cures will be performed by things which are

not repulsive to the smell and taste of man—that is to
say, by aliments, fruits and vegetables which are agreeable
to the taste and have an agreeable smell. 7

Should ye be attacked by illness or disease, consult
skillful physicians. 8

It is incumbent upon everyone to seek medical treatment
and to follow the doctor's instructions, for this is in
compliance with the divine ordinance, but, in reality, He
Who giveth healing is God. 9

Do not neglect medical treatment when it is necessary,
but leave it off when health has been restored. Treat
disease through diet, by preference, refraining from the
use of drugs; and if you find what is required in a single
herb, do not resort to a compounded medicament. . . .
Abstain from drugs when the health is good, but admin-
ister them when necessary. 10

All true healing comes from God! There are two causes
for sickness; one is material, the other spiritual. If the
sickness is of the body, a material remedy is needed, if of
the soul, a spiritual remedy.
   If the heavenly benediction be upon us while we are
being healed, then only can we be made whole, for
medicine is but the outward and visible means through
which we obtain the heavenly healing. Unless the
spirit be healed, the cure of the body is worth nothing.
All is in the hands of God, and without Him there
can be no health in us! 11

Guidance for Physicians

TURN thou toward God with thy heart throbbing
with His love, devoted to His praise, gazing toward
His kingdom and seeking help from His Holy Spirit in a
state of ecstasy, rapture, love, yearning, joy and fragrance.

Then will God assist thee, through a Spirit from His
Presence, to heal sickness and disease. 12

O physicians! In treating the sick, first mention the name
of thy God, the Possessor of the Day of Judgment, and
then use what God hath destined for the healing of His
creatures. By My Life! The physician who has drunk
from the Wine of My Love, his visit is healing, and his
breath is mercy and hope. Cling to him for the welfare of
the constitution. He is confirmed by God in his
treatment.
    This knowledge is the most important of all the
sciences, for it is the greatest means from God, the Life-
giver to the dust, for preserving the bodies of all people,
and He has put it in the forefront of all sciences and
wisdoms. 13

O thou distinguished physician! . . . Praise be to God
that thou hast two powers: one to undertake physical
healing and the other spiritual healing. Matters related to
man's spirit have a great effect on his bodily condition.
For instance, thou shouldst impart gladness to thy
patient, give him comfort and joy, and bring him to
ecstasy and exultation. How often hath it occurred that
this hath caused early recovery. Therefore, treat thou the
sick with both powers. Spiritual feelings have a surpris-
ing effect on healing nervous ailments. 14

When giving medical treatment, turn to the Blessed
Beauty,* then follow the dictates of thy heart. Remedy
the sick by means of heavenly joy and spiritual exultation, cure the sorely afflicted by imparting to them
blissful glad tidings and heal the wounded through His
resplendent bestowals. When at the bedside of a patient,
cheer and gladden his heart and enrapture his spirit
through celestial power. Indeed, such a heavenly breath

---
*Bahá'u'lláh.

quickeneth every moldering bone and reviveth the spirit
of every sick and ailing one. **15**

The Means of Preserving Health

B E THE essence of cleanliness among mankind . . .
under all circumstances conform yourselves to
refined manners . . . let no trace of uncleanliness appear
on your clothes. . . . Immerse yourselves in pure water; a
water which hath been used is not allowable. . . . Verily,
We have desired to see in you the manifestations of
Paradise on earth, so that there may be diffused from
you that whereat the hearts of the favored ones shall
rejoice. **16**

Although bodily cleanliness is a physical thing, it hath,
nevertheless, a powerful influence on the life of the
spirit. It is even as a voice wondrously sweet, or a melody
played: Although sounds are but vibrations in the air
which affect the ear's auditory nerve, and these vibrations
are but chance phenomena carried along through the
air, even so, see how they move the heart. A wondrous
melody is wings for the spirit, and maketh the soul
to tremble for joy. The purport is that physical cleanliness doth also exert its effect upon the human soul.

Observe how pleasing is cleanliness in the sight of
God, and how specifically it is emphasized in the Holy
Books of the Prophets; for the Scriptures forbid the
eating or the use of any unclean thing. Some of these
prohibitions were absolute, and binding upon all, and
whoso transgressed the given law was abhorred of God
and anathematized by the believers. . . .

But there are other forbidden things which do not
cause immediate harm, and the injurious effects of which
are only gradually produced: Such acts are also repug-
nant to the Lord, and blameworthy in His sight, and
repellant. The absolute unlawfulness of these, however,
hath not been expressly set forth in the Text, but their

avoidance is necessary to purity, cleanliness, the preservation of health, and freedom from addiction.

Among these latter is smoking tobacco, which is dirty, smelly, offensive—an evil habit, and one the harmfulness of which gradually becometh apparent to all. **17**

The drinking of wine . . . is the cause of chronic diseases, weakeneth the nerves, and consumeth the mind. **18**

O ye, God's loved ones! Experience hath shown how greatly the renouncing of smoking, of intoxicating drink, and of opium, conduceth to health and vigor, to the expansion and keenness of the mind and to bodily strength. **19**

Verily, the most necessary thing is contentment under all circumstances; by this one is preserved from morbid conditions and from lassitude. Yield not to grief and sorrow; they cause the greatest misery. Jealousy consumeth the body and anger doth burn the liver; avoid these two as you would a lion. **20**

I hope thou wilt become as a rising light and obtain spiritual health—and spiritual health is conducive to physical health. . . . **21**

Praying for Healing

O HANDMAID of God! The prayers which were revealed to ask for healing apply both to physical and spiritual healing. Recite them, then, to heal both the soul and the body. If healing is right for the patient, it will certainly be granted; but for some ailing persons, healing would only be the cause of other ills, and, therefore, wisdom doth not permit an affirmative answer to the prayer.

O handmaid of God! The power of the Holy Spirit healeth both physical and spiritual ailments. **22**

Thy name is my healing, O my God, and remembrance of Thee is my remedy. Nearness to Thee is my hope, and love for Thee is my companion. Thy mercy to me is my healing and my succor in both this world and the world to come. Thou, verily, art the All-Bountiful, the All-Knowing, the All-Wise.   23

13

Marriage and Family Life

The Nature of Marriage

FROM separation doth every kind of hurt and harm
proceed, but the union of created things doth
ever yield most laudable results. From the pairing of
even the smallest particles in the world of being are the
grace and bounty of God made manifest; and the higher
the degree, the more momentous is the union. . . . And
above all other unions is that between human beings,
especially when it cometh to pass in the love of God.
Thus is the primal oneness made to appear; thus is laid
the foundation of love in the spirit.   1

Marriage, among the mass of the people, is a physical
bond, and this union can only be temporary, since it
is foredoomed to a physical separation at the close.
Among the people of Bahá,* however, marriage must
be a union of the body and of the spirit as well, for
here both husband and wife are aglow with the same
wine; both are enamored of the same matchless Face;
both live and move through the same spirit; both are
illumined by the same glory. This connection between
them is a spiritual one; hence it is a bond that will abide
forever. Likewise do they enjoy strong and lasting ties
in the physical world as well, for if the marriage is based
both on the spirit and the body, that union is a true
one; hence it will endure. If, however, the bond is
physical and nothing more, it is sure to be only temporary, and must inexorably end in separation.

---

*Bahá'ís, followers of Bahá'u'lláh.

When, therefore, the people of Bahá undertake to
marry, the union must be a true relationship, a spiritual
coming together as well as a physical one, so that
throughout every phase of life, and in all the worlds of
God, their union will endure; for this real oneness is
a gleaming out of the love of God.   2

Bahá'í marriage is the commitment of the two parties
one to the other, and their mutual attachment of mind
and heart. Each must, however, exercise the utmost care
to become thoroughly acquainted with the character
of the other, that the binding covenant between them
may be a tie that will endure forever. Their purpose must
be this: to become loving companions and comrades
and at one with each other for time and eternity. . . .
   The true marriage of Bahá'ís is this, that husband and
wife should be united both physically and spiritually,
that they may ever improve the spiritual life of each
other, and may enjoy everlasting unity throughout all the
worlds of God. This is Bahá'í marriage.   3

O ye two believers in God! The Lord, peerless is He,
hath made woman and man to abide with each other in
the closest companionship, and to be even as a single
soul. They are two helpmates, two intimate friends, who
should be concerned about the welfare of each other.
   If they live thus, they will pass through this world
with perfect contentment, bliss, and peace of heart, and
become the object of divine grace and favor in the
kingdom of heaven. But if they do other than this, they
will live out their lives in great bitterness, longing at
every moment for death, and will be shamefaced in the
heavenly realm.
   Strive, then, to abide, heart and soul, with each other
as two doves in the nest, for this is to be blessed in
both worlds.   4

The importance of marriage lieth in the bringing up of a

richly blessed family, so that with entire gladness they
may, even as candles, illuminate the world. For the
enlightenment of the world dependeth upon the existence of man. If man did not exist in this world, it would
have been like a tree without fruit.   5

It is highly important for man to raise a family. So long
as he is young, because of youthful self-complacency,
he does not realize its significance, but this will be a
source of regret when he grows old. . . . In this glorious
Cause the life of a married couple should resemble the
life of the angels in heaven—a life full of joy and spiritual delight, a life of unity and concord, a friendship both
mental and physical. The home should be orderly and
well organized. Their ideas and thoughts should be like
the rays of the sun of truth and the radiance of the
brilliant stars in the heavens. Even as two birds they
should warble melodies upon the branches of the tree of
fellowship and harmony. They should always be elated
with joy and gladness and be a source of happiness to the
hearts of others. They should set an example to their
fellowmen, manifest true and sincere love towards each
other and educate their children in such a manner as
to blazon the fame and glory of their family.   6

The Rearing of Children

AMONG the greatest of all services that can possibly
be rendered by man to Almighty God is the education and training of children. . . .   7

Were there no educator, all souls would remain savage,
and were it not for the teacher, the children would be
ignorant creatures.

It is for this reason that, in this new cycle, education
and training are recorded in the Book of God as
obligatory and not voluntary. That is, it is enjoined upon
the father and mother, as a duty, to strive with all effort

to train the daughter and the son, to nurse them from the breast of knowledge and to rear them in the bosom of sciences and arts. Should they neglect this matter, they shall be held responsible and worthy of reproach in the presence of the stern Lord.   **8**

From the very beginning, the children must receive divine education and must continually be reminded to remember their God. Let the love of God pervade their inmost being, commingled with their mother's milk.   **9**

Teach your children what hath been revealed through the Pen of Glory. Instruct them in what hath descended from the heaven of greatness and power. Let them memorize the Tablets of the Merciful and chant them with the most melodious voices. . . .   **10**

The parents must exert every effort to rear their offspring to be religious, for should the children not attain this greatest of adornments, they will not obey their parents, which in a certain sense means that they will not obey God. Indeed, such children will show no consideration to anyone, and will do exactly as they please.   **11**

As to thy question regarding the education of children: It behooveth thee to nurture them at the breast of the love of God, and urge them onward to the things of the spirit, that they may turn their faces unto God; that their ways may conform to the rules of good conduct and their character be second to none; that they make their own all the graces and praiseworthy qualities of humankind; acquire a sound knowledge of the various branches of learning, so that from the very beginning of life they may become spiritual beings, dwellers in the kingdom, enamored of the sweet breaths of holiness, and may receive an education religious, spiritual, and of the heavenly realm.   **12**

While the children are yet in their infancy feed them from the breast of heavenly grace, foster them in the cradle of all excellence, rear them in the embrace of bounty. Give them the advantage of every useful kind of knowledge. Let them share in every new and rare and wondrous craft and art. Bring them up to work and strive, and accustom them to hardship. Teach them to dedicate their lives to matters of great import, and inspire them to undertake studies that will benefit mankind.   13

Training in morals and good conduct is far more important than book learning. A child that is cleanly, agreeable, of good character, well behaved—even though
he be ignorant—is preferable to a child that is rude,
unwashed, ill natured, and yet becoming deeply versed in
all the sciences and arts. The reason for this is that the
child who conducts himself well, even though he be
ignorant, is of benefit to others, while an ill-natured, ill-
behaved child is corrupted and harmful to others, even
though he be learned. If, however, the child be trained to
be both learned and good, the result is light upon light.
    Children are even as a branch that is fresh and green;
they will grow up in whatever way ye train them.
Take the utmost care to give them high ideals and goals,
so that once they come of age, they will cast their
beams like brilliant candles on the world, and will not be
defiled by lusts and passions in the way of animals,
heedless and unaware, but instead will set their hearts on
achieving everlasting honor and acquiring all the excel-
lences of humankind.   14

Prayers for Infants, Children, and Youth

PRAISED be Thou, O Lord my God! Graciously grant
that this infant be fed from the breast of Thy
tender mercy and loving providence and be nourished
with the fruit of Thy celestial trees. Suffer him not to be

committed to the care of anyone save Thee, inasmuch as Thou, Thyself, through the potency of Thy sovereign will and power, didst create and call him into being. There is none other God but Thee, the Almighty, the All-Knowing.

Lauded art Thou, O my Best Beloved. Waft over him the sweet savors of Thy transcendent bounty and the fragrances of Thy holy bestowals. Enable him then to seek shelter beneath the shadow of Thy most exalted Name, O Thou Who holdest in Thy grasp the kingdom of names and attributes. Verily, Thou art potent to do what Thou willest, and Thou art, indeed, the Mighty, the Exalted, the Ever-Forgiving, the Gracious, the Generous, the Merciful.   15

O Lord! Help this daughter of the kingdom to be exalted in both worlds; cause her to turn away from this mortal world of dust and from those who have set their hearts thereon and enable her to have communion and close association with the world of immortality. Give her heavenly power and strengthen her through the breaths of the Holy Spirit that she may arise to serve Thee.

Thou art the Mighty One.   16

O Lord! Make this youth radiant, and confer Thy bounty upon this poor creature. Bestow upon him knowledge, grant him added strength at the break of every morn and guard him within the shelter of Thy protection so that he may be freed from error, may devote himself to the service of Thy Cause, may guide the wayward, lead the hapless, free the captives and awaken the heedless, that all may be blessed with Thy remembrance and praise. Thou art the Mighty and the Powerful.   17

The Station of Motherhood

O HANDMAID of God! . . . To the mothers must be given the divine teachings and effective counsel, and they must be encouraged and made eager to train their children, for the mother is the first educator of the child. It is she who must, at the very beginning, suckle the newborn at the breast of God's Faith and God's Law, that divine love may enter into him even with his mother's milk, and be with him till his final breath.

So long as the mother faileth to train her children, and start them on a proper way of life, the training which they receive later on will not take its full effect. 18

For mothers are the first educators, the first mentors; and truly it is the mothers who determine the happiness, the future greatness, the courteous ways and learning and judgment, the understanding and the faith of their little ones. 19

The question of training the children and looking after the orphans is extremely important, but most important of all is the education of girl children, for these girls will one day be mothers, and the mother is the first teacher of the child. In whatever way she reareth the child, so will the child become, and the results of that first training will remain with the individual throughout his entire life, and it would be most difficult to alter them. And how can a mother, herself ignorant and untrained, educate her child? It is, therefore, clear that the education of girls is of far greater consequence than that of boys. This fact is extremely important, and the matter must be seen to with the greatest energy and dedication. 20

Relationships within the Family

ACCORDING to the teachings of Bahá'u'lláh the family, being a human unit, must be educated according to the rules of sanctity. All the virtues must be taught the family. The integrity of the family bond must be constantly considered, and the rights of the

individual members must not be transgressed. The rights
of the son, the father, the mother—none of them must
be transgressed, none of them must be arbitrary. Just
as the son has certain obligations to his father, the father,
likewise, has certain obligations to his son. The mother,
the sister and other members of the household have
their certain prerogatives. All these rights and prerogatives must be conserved, yet the unity of the family must
be sustained. The injury of one shall be considered the
injury of all; the comfort of each, the comfort of all; the
honor of one, the honor of all.   21

The father must always endeavor to educate his son and
to acquaint him with the heavenly teachings. He must
give him advice and exhort him at all times, teach
him praiseworthy conduct and character, enable him to
receive training at school and to be instructed in such
arts and sciences as are deemed useful and necessary. In
brief, let him instill into his mind the virtues and perfections of the world of humanity. Above all he should
continually call to his mind the remembrance of God so
that his throbbing veins and arteries may pulsate with
the love of God.

The son, on the other hand, must show forth the
utmost obedience towards his father, and should conduct
himself as a humble and a lowly servant. Day and night
he should seek diligently to ensure the comfort and
welfare of his loving father and to secure his good
pleasure. He must forgo his own rest and enjoyment, and
constantly strive to bring gladness to the hearts of his
father and mother, that thereby he may attain the good
pleasure of the Almighty and be graciously aided by the
hosts of the unseen.   22

Say, O My people! Show honor to your parents and pay
homage to them. This will cause blessings to descend
upon you from the clouds of the bounty of your Lord, the
Exalted, the Great. . . .

Beware lest ye commit that which would sadden the hearts of your fathers and mothers. Follow ye the path of Truth which, indeed, is a straight path. Should anyone give you a choice between the opportunity to render a service to Me and a service to them, choose ye to serve them, and let such service be a path leading you to Me. This is My exhortation and command unto thee. Observe, therefore, that which thy Lord, the Mighty, the Gracious, hath prescribed unto thee.   23

Also a father and mother endure the greatest troubles and hardships for their children; and often when the children have reached the age of maturity, the parents pass on to the other world. Rarely does it happen that a father and mother in this world see the reward of the care and trouble they have undergone for their children. Therefore, children, in return for this care and trouble, must show forth charity and beneficence, and must implore pardon and forgiveness for their parents. So you ought, in return for the love and kindness shown you by your father, to give to the poor for his sake, with greatest submission and humility implore pardon and remission of sins, and ask for the supreme mercy.   24

The Spiritual Home

EXALTED art Thou, O Lord God. Let Thy heavenly blessings descend upon homes whose inmates have believed in Thee. Verily, unsurpassed art Thou in sending down divine blessings.   25

Blessed is the house that hath attained unto My tender mercy, wherein My remembrance is celebrated, and which is ennobled by the presence of My loved ones, who have proclaimed My praise, cleaved fast to the cord of My grace and been honored by chanting My verses. 26

I beseech God to graciously make of thy home a center

for the diffusion of the light of divine guidance, for the dissemination of the Words of God and for enkindling at all times the fire of love in the hearts of His faithful servants and maidservants. Know thou of a certainty that every house wherein the anthem of praise is raised to the Realm of Glory in celebration of the Name of God is, indeed, a heavenly home, and one of the gardens of delight in the paradise of God.　27

14

Love and Fellowship

The Bond of Love

IF THE learned and worldly wise men of this age were to allow mankind to inhale the fragrance of fellowship and love, every understanding heart would apprehend the meaning of true liberty, and discover the secret of undisturbed peace and absolute composure. 1

Know thou of a certainty that love is the secret of God's holy dispensation, the manifestation of the All-Merciful, the fountain of spiritual outpourings. Love is heaven's kindly light, the Holy Spirit's eternal breath that vivifieth the human soul. Love is the cause of God's revelation unto man, the vital bond inherent, in accordance with the divine creation, in the realities of things. Love is the one means that ensureth true felicity both in this world and the next. Love is the light that guideth in darkness, the living link that uniteth God with man, that assureth the progress of every illumined soul. Love is the most great law that ruleth this mighty and heavenly cycle, the unique power that bindeth together the divers elements of this material world, the supreme magnetic force that directeth the movements of the spheres in the celestial realms. Love revealeth with unfailing and limitless power the mysteries latent in the universe. Love is the spirit of life unto the adorned body of mankind, the establisher of true civilization in this mortal world, and the shedder of imperishable glory upon every high-aiming race and nation.

Whatsoever people is graciously favored therewith by God, its name shall surely be magnified and extolled by the Concourse from on high, by the company of angels, and the denizens of the Abhá Kingdom.* And whatsoever people turneth its heart away from this divine love—the revelation of the Merciful—shall err grievously, shall fall into despair, and be utterly destroyed. That people shall be denied all refuge, shall become even as the vilest creatures of the earth, victims of degradation and shame.

O ye beloved of the Lord! Strive to become the manifestations of the love of God, the lamps of divine guidance shining amongst the kindreds of the earth with the light of love and concord.   2

When you love a member of your family or a compatriot, let it be with a ray of the Infinite Love! Let it be in God, and for God! Wherever you find the attributes of God, love that person, whether he be of your family or of another.   3

All-Embracing Love and Unity

O YE beloved of the Lord! This day is the day of union, the day of the ingathering of all mankind.   4

O ye loved ones of the Lord! This is the hour when ye must associate with all the earth's peoples in extreme kindliness and love, and be to them the signs and tokens of God's great mercy. Ye must become the very soul of the world, the living spirit in the body of the children of men.   5

O ye beloved of God! Know ye, verily, that the happiness of mankind lieth in the unity and the harmony of the

_____

*The kingdom of God. *Abhá* means "Most Glorious."

human race, and that spiritual and material developments
are conditioned upon love and amity among all men.   6

Now is the time for the lovers of God to raise high
the banners of unity, to intone, in the assemblages of the
world, the verses of friendship and love and to demonstrate to all that the grace of God is one. Thus will
the tabernacles of holiness be upraised on the summits of
the earth, gathering all peoples into the protective
shadow of the Word of Oneness. This great bounty will
dawn over the world at the time when the lovers of
God shall arise to carry out His teachings, and to scatter
far and wide the fresh, sweet scents of universal love.

In every dispensation there hath been the commandment of fellowship and love, but it was a commandment
limited to the community of those in mutual agreement,
not to the dissident foe. In this wondrous age, however,
praised be God, the commandments of God are not
delimited, not restricted to any one group of people;
rather have all the friends been commanded to show
forth fellowship and love, consideration and generosity
and loving kindness to every community on earth. Now
must the lovers of God arise to carry out these instructions of His: Let them be kindly fathers to the children of
the human race, and compassionate brothers to the
youth, and self-denying offspring to those bent with
years. The meaning of this is that ye must show forth
tenderness and love to every human being, even to your
enemies, and welcome them all with unalloyed friendship, good cheer, and loving kindness.   7

Consort with the followers of all religions in a spirit of
friendliness and fellowship. . . .

They that are endued with sincerity and faithfulness
should associate with all the peoples and kindreds of the
earth with joy and radiance, inasmuch as consorting
with people hath promoted and will continue to promote

unity and concord, which in turn are conducive to the maintenance of order in the world and to the regeneration of nations. Blessed are such as hold fast to the cord of kindliness and tender mercy and are free from animosity and hatred.   8

Of old it hath been revealed: "Love of one's country is an element of the Faith of God." The Tongue of Grandeur hath, however, in the day of His manifestation proclaimed: "It is not his to boast who loveth his country, but it is his who loveth the world." Through the power released by these exalted words He hath lent a fresh impulse, and set a new direction, to the birds of men's hearts, and hath obliterated every trace of restriction and limitation from God's holy Book.   9

We have created you from one tree and have caused you to be as the leaves and fruit of the same tree, that haply ye may become a source of comfort to one another. Regard ye not others save as ye regard your own selves, that no feeling of aversion may prevail amongst you. . . . It behooveth you all to be one indivisible people. . . .   10

Achieving Harmony with Diversity

A CRITIC may object, saying that peoples, races, tribes and communities of the world are of different and varied customs, habits, tastes, character, inclinations and ideas, that opinions and thoughts are contrary to one another, and how, therefore, is it possible for real unity to be revealed and perfect accord among human souls to exist?

In answer we say that differences are of two kinds. One is the cause of annihilation and is like the antipathy existing among warring nations and conflicting tribes who seek each other's destruction, uprooting one another's families, depriving one another of rest and comfort

and unleashing carnage. The other kind which is a token
of diversity is the essence of perfection and the cause of
the appearance of the bestowals of the Most Glorious
Lord.

Consider the flowers of a garden: Though differing in
kind, color, form and shape, yet, inasmuch as they are
refreshed by the waters of one spring, revived by the
breath of one wind, invigorated by the rays of one sun,
this diversity increaseth their charm, and addeth unto
their beauty. Thus when that unifying force, the penetrating influence of the Word of God, taketh effect,
the difference of customs, manners, habits, ideas, opinions and dispositions embellisheth the world of humanity. This diversity, this difference is like the naturally
created dissimilarity and variety of the limbs and organs
of the human body, for each one contributeth to the
beauty, efficiency and perfection of the whole. When
these different limbs and organs come under the influence of man's sovereign soul, and the soul's power
pervadeth the limbs and members, veins and arteries of
the body, then difference reinforceth harmony, diversity
strengtheneth love, and multiplicity is the greatest
factor for coordination.

How unpleasing to the eye if all the flowers and
plants, the leaves and blossoms, the fruits, the branches
and the trees of that garden were all of the same shape
and color! Diversity of hues, form and shape, enricheth
and adorneth the garden, and heighteneth the effect
thereof. In like manner, when divers shades of thought,
temperament and character are brought together under
the power and influence of one central agency, the
beauty and glory of human perfection will be revealed
and made manifest. Naught but the celestial potency of
the Word of God, which ruleth and transcendeth the
realities of all things, is capable of harmonizing the
divergent thoughts, sentiments, ideas, and convictions of
the children of men. Verily, it is the penetrating power

in all things, the mover of souls and the binder and
regulator in the world of humanity.   11

The diversity in the human family should be the cause of
love and harmony, as it is in music where many different
notes blend together in the making of a perfect chord.
If you meet those of different race and color from yourself, do not mistrust them and withdraw yourself into
your shell of conventionality, but, rather, be glad and
show them kindness. Think of them as different colored
roses growing in the beautiful garden of humanity, and
rejoice to be among them.   12

There are no whites and blacks before God. All colors
are one, and that is the color of servitude to God. Scent
and color are not important. The heart is important.
If the heart is pure, white or black or any color makes no
difference. God does not look at colors; He looks at the
hearts. He whose heart is pure is better. He whose
character is better is more pleasing. He who turns more
to the Abhá Kingdom* is more advanced.
     In the realm of existence colors are of no importance. 13

When the racial elements of the American nation unite
in actual fellowship and accord, the lights of the oneness
of humanity will shine, the day of eternal glory and
bliss will dawn, the spirit of God encompass, and the
divine favors descend. Under the leadership and training
of God, the real Shepherd, all will be protected and
preserved. He will lead them in green pastures of happiness and sustenance, and they will attain to the real
goal of existence. This is the blessing and benefit of
unity; this is the outcome of love. This is the sign of the
Most Great Peace; this is the star of the oneness of the
human world.   14

---

*The kingdom of God. *Abhá* means "Most Glorious."

Humanity's Lack of Genuine Love and Fellowship

THE great mass of humanity does not exercise real love and fellowship. The elect of humanity are those who live together in love and unity. They are preferable before God because the divine attributes are already manifest in them.   15

Although the body politic is one family, yet because of lack of harmonious relations some members are comfortable and some in direst misery, some members are satisfied and some are hungry, some members are clothed in most costly garments and some families are in need of food and shelter. Why? Because this family lacks the necessary reciprocity and symmetry. This household is not well arranged. . . .

Is it possible for one member of a family to be subjected to the utmost misery and to abject poverty and for the rest of the family to be comfortable? It is impossible unless those members of the family be senseless, atrophied, inhospitable, unkind.   16

The disease which afflicts the body politic is lack of love and absence of altruism. In the hearts of men no real love is found, and the condition is such that, unless their susceptibilities are quickened by some power so that unity, love and accord may develop within them, there can be no healing, no agreement among mankind. Love and unity are the needs of the body politic today. Without these there can be no progress or prosperity attained. Therefore, the friends of God must adhere to the power which will create this love and unity in the hearts of the sons of men. Science cannot cure the illness of the body politic. Science cannot create amity and fellowship in human hearts. Neither can patriotism nor racial allegiance effect a remedy. It must be accomplished solely through the divine bounties and spiritual bestowals

which have descended from God in this day for that
purpose. This is an exigency of the times, and the divine
remedy has been provided. The spiritual teachings of
the religion of God can alone create this love, unity and
accord in human hearts.   17

Religion—The Cause of Love and Unity

FOR a single purpose were the prophets, each and all,
sent down to earth; for this was Christ made
manifest, for this did Bahá'u'lláh raise up the call of the
Lord: that the world of man should become the world of
God, this nether realm the kingdom, this darkness
light, this satanic wickedness all the virtues of heaven—
and unity, fellowship and love be won for the whole
human race, that the organic unity should reappear and
the bases of discord be destroyed and life everlasting
and grace everlasting become the harvest of mankind.   18

Religion must be the cause of fellowship and love. If it
become the cause of estrangement, then it is not needed,
for religion is like a remedy; if it aggravate the disease,
then it becometh unnecessary.   19

The purpose of religion as revealed from the heaven of
God's holy Will is to establish unity and concord
amongst the peoples of the world; make it not the cause
of dissension and strife. The religion of God and His
divine law are the most potent instruments and the surest
of all means for the dawning of the light of unity
amongst men. The progress of the world, the development of nations, the tranquillity of peoples, and the
peace of all who dwell on earth are among the principles
and ordinances of God. Religion bestoweth upon man
the most precious of all gifts, offereth the cup of prosperity, imparteth eternal life, and showereth imperishable
benefits upon mankind.   20

The holy Manifestations of God were sent down to make visible the oneness of humanity. For this did They endure unnumbered ills and tribulations, that a community from amongst mankind's divergent peoples could gather within the shadow of the Word of God and live as one, and could, with delight and grace, demonstrate on earth the unity of humankind. Therefore must the desire of the friends be this, to bring together and unify all peoples, that all may receive a generous drink of this pure wine. . . .   21

The great and fundamental teachings of Bahá'u'lláh are the oneness of God and unity of mankind. This is the bond of union among Bahá'ís all over the world. They become united among themselves, then unite others. It is impossible to unite unless united.   22

Become as true brethren in the one and indivisible religion of God, free from distinction, for, verily, God desireth that your hearts should become mirrors unto your brethren in the Faith, so that ye find yourselves reflected in them, and they in you. This is the true Path of God, the Almighty, and He is, indeed, watchful over your actions.   23

How good it is if the friends be as close as sheaves of light, if they stand together side by side in a firm, unbroken line. For now have the rays of reality from the Sun of the world of existence united in adoration all the worshipers of this light; and these rays have, through infinite grace, gathered all peoples together within this wide-spreading shelter; therefore, must all souls become as one soul, and all hearts as one heart. Let all be set free from the multiple identities that were born of passion and desire, and in the oneness of their love for God find a new way of life.   24

Wherefore must the friends of God, with utter sanctity, with one accord, rise up in the spirit, in unity with one another, to such a degree that they will become even as one being and one soul. On such a plane as this, physical bodies play no part; rather doth the spirit take over and rule; and when its power encompasseth all, then is spiritual union achieved. Strive ye by day and night to cultivate your unity to the fullest degree. 25

Fostering and Preserving Fellowship

THE advent of the prophets and the revelation of the Holy Books are intended to create love between souls and friendship among the inhabitants of the earth. Real love is impossible unless one turn his face towards God and be attracted to His Beauty. 26

O ye lovers of this wronged one! Cleanse ye your eyes so that ye behold no man as different from yourselves. See ye no strangers; rather, see all men as friends, for love and unity come hard when ye fix your gaze on otherness. And in this new and wondrous age, the holy Writings say that we must be at one with every people; that we must see neither harshness nor injustice, neither malevolence, nor hostility, nor hate, but, rather, turn our eyes toward the heaven of ancient glory. For each of the creatures is a sign of God, and it was by the grace of the Lord and His power that each did step into the world; therefore, they are not strangers, but in the family; not aliens, but friends, and to be treated as such.

Wherefore must the loved ones of God associate in affectionate fellowship with stranger and friend alike, showing forth to all the utmost loving kindness, disregarding the degree of their capacity, never asking whether they deserve to be loved. In every instance let the friends be considerate and infinitely kind. Let them never be defeated by the malice of the people, by their aggression and their hate, no matter how intense. If others hurl their darts against you, offer them milk and honey in return; if they poison your lives, sweeten their souls; if they injure you, teach them how to be comforted; if they inflict a wound upon you, be a balm to their sores; if they sting you, hold to their lips a refreshing cup.   27

Be most loving one to another. Burn away, wholly for the sake of the Well-Beloved, the veil of self with the flame of the undying Fire, and with faces joyous and beaming with light, associate with your neighbors.   28

Let not conventionality cause you to seem cold and unsympathetic when you meet strange people from other countries. Do not look at them as though you suspected them of being evil-doers, thieves and boors. You think it necessary to be very careful, not to expose yourselves to the risk of making acquaintance with such, possibly, undesirable people.

I ask you not to think only of yourselves. Be kind to the strangers, whether come they from Turkey, Japan, Persia, Russia, China or any other country in the world.

Help to make them feel at home; find out where they are staying; ask if you may render them any service; try to make their lives a little happier.

In this way, even if, sometimes, what you at first suspected should be true, still go out of your way to be kind to them—this kindness will help them to become better. . . .

Let those who meet you know, without your pro-claiming the fact, that you are indeed a Bahá'í.

Put into practice the teaching of Bahá'u'lláh, that of kindness to all nations. Do not be content with showing friendship in words alone; let your heart burn with loving kindness for all who may cross your path. . . .

What profit is there in agreeing that universal friendship is good, and talking of the solidarity of the human race as a grand ideal? Unless these thoughts are translated into the world of action, they are useless.

The wrong in the world continues to exist just because people talk only of their ideals, and do not strive to put them into practice. If actions took the place of words, the world's misery would very soon be changed into comfort.   29

Consort with all men, O people of Bahá,* in a spirit of friendliness and fellowship. If ye be aware of a certain truth, if ye possess a jewel, of which others are deprived, share it with them in a language of utmost kindliness and goodwill. If it be accepted, if it fulfill its purpose, your object is attained. If anyone should refuse it, leave him unto himself, and beseech God to guide him. Beware lest ye deal unkindly with him. A kindly tongue is the lodestone of the hearts of men. It is the bread of the spirit; it clotheth the words with meaning; it is the fountain of the light of wisdom and understanding. . . .   30

When you meet those whose opinions differ from your own, do not turn away your face from them. All are seeking truth, and there are many roads leading thereto. Truth has many aspects, but it remains always and forever one.

Do not allow difference of opinion, or diversity of thought, to separate you from your fellowmen, or to be the cause of dispute, hatred and strife in your hearts.

Rather, search diligently for the truth, and make all men your friends.   31

Be in perfect unity. Never become angry with one another. Let your eyes be directed toward the kingdom of truth and not toward the world of creation. Love the

---

*Bahá'ís, followers of Bahá'u'lláh.

creatures for the sake of God and not for themselves. You will never become angry or impatient if you love them for the sake of God. Humanity is not perfect. There are imperfections in every human being, and you will always become unhappy if you look toward the people themselves. But if you look toward God, you will love them and be kind to them, for the world of God is the world of perfection and complete mercy. Therefore, do not look at the shortcomings of anybody; see with the sight of forgiveness. The imperfect eye beholds imperfections. The eye that covers faults looks toward the Creator of souls. He created them, trains and provides for them, endows them with capacity and life, sight and hearing; therefore, they are the signs of His grandeur.   32

O beloved of the Lord! If any soul speak ill of an absent one, the only result will clearly be this: He will dampen the zeal of the friends and tend to make them indifferent. For backbiting is divisive; it is the leading cause among the friends of a disposition to withdraw. If any individual should speak ill of one who is absent, it is incumbent on his hearers, in a spiritual and friendly manner, to stop him, and say in effect: Would this detraction serve any useful purpose? Would it please the Blessed Beauty, contribute to the lasting honor of the friends, promote the holy Faith, support the Covenant, or be of any possible benefit to any soul? No, never! On the contrary, it would make the dust to settle so thickly on the heart that the ears would hear no more, and the eyes would no longer behold the light of truth.

If, however, a person setteth about speaking well of another, opening his lips to praise another, he will touch an answering chord in his hearers, and they will be stirred up by the breathings of God.   33

O army of God! Beware lest ye harm any soul, or make any heart to sorrow; lest ye wound any man with your words, be he known to you or a stranger, be he friend or

foe. Pray ye for all; ask ye that all be blessed, all be
forgiven. Beware, beware, lest any of you seek ven-
geance, even against one who is thirsting for your blood.
Beware, beware, lest ye offend the feelings of another,
even though he be an evildoer, and he wish you ill. Look
ye not upon the creatures; turn ye to their Creator. See
ye not the never-yielding people; see but the Lord of
Hosts. Gaze ye not down upon the dust; gaze upward at
the shining sun, which hath caused every patch of
darksome earth to glow with light.   34

I charge you all that each one of you concentrate all the
thoughts of your heart on love and unity. When a
thought of war comes, oppose it by a stronger thought of
peace. A thought of hatred must be destroyed by a more
powerful thought of love. Thoughts of war bring destruction to all harmony, well-being, restfulness and
content.

Thoughts of love are constructive of brotherhood,
peace, friendship, and happiness. . . .

If you desire with all your heart friendship with every
race on earth, your thought, spiritual and positive, will
spread; it will become the desire of others, growing
stronger and stronger, until it reaches the minds of all
men.   35

Prayers for Love and Unity

O GOD, my God! Aid Thou Thy trusted servants to
have loving and tender hearts. Help them to
spread, amongst all the nations of the earth, the light of
guidance that cometh from the Company on high.
Verily, Thou art the Strong, the Powerful, the Mighty,
the All-Subduing, the Ever-Giving. Verily, Thou art the
Generous, the Gentle, the Tender, the Most Bountiful. 36

O Thou compassionate Lord, Thou Who art generous
and able! We are servants of Thine sheltered beneath

Thy providence. Cast Thy glance of favor upon us. Give
light to our eyes, hearing to our ears, and understanding
and love to our hearts. Render our souls joyous and
happy through Thy glad tidings. O Lord! Point out to us
the pathway of Thy kingdom and resuscitate all of us
through the breaths of the Holy Spirit. Bestow upon us
life everlasting and confer upon us never-ending honor.
Unify mankind and illumine the world of humanity.
May we all follow Thy pathway, long for Thy good
pleasure and seek the mysteries of Thy kingdom. O God!
Unite us and connect our hearts with Thy indissoluble
bond. Verily, Thou art the Giver, Thou art the Kind One
and Thou art the Almighty.   37

O Thou kind Lord! Thou hast created all humanity from
the same stock. Thou hast decreed that all shall belong
to the same household. In Thy holy Presence they are all
Thy servants, and all mankind are sheltered beneath
Thy Tabernacle; all have gathered together at Thy Table
of Bounty; all are illumined through the light of Thy
Providence.

O God! Thou art kind to all. Thou hast provided for
all, dost shelter all, conferrest life upon all. Thou hast
endowed each and all with talents and faculties, and all
are submerged in the Ocean of Thy Mercy.

O Thou kind Lord! Unite all. Let the religions agree
and make the nations one, so that they may see each
other as one family and the whole earth as one home.
May they all live together in perfect harmony.

O God! Raise aloft the banner of the oneness of
mankind.

O God! Establish the Most Great Peace.

Cement Thou, O God, the hearts together.

O Thou kind Father, God! Gladden our hearts
through the fragrance of Thy love. Brighten our eyes
through the Light of Thy Guidance. Delight our ears
with the melody of Thy Word, and shelter us all in the
Stronghold of Thy Providence.

Thou art the Mighty and Powerful, Thou art the Forgiving and Thou art the One Who overlooketh the shortcomings of all mankind.   38

15

Peace and Unity

Turning from War to Peace

WAR and rapine with their attendant cruelties are an abomination to God, and bring their own punishment, for the God of love is also a God of justice, and each man must inevitably reap what he sows.   1

War is destruction while universal peace is construction; war is death while peace is life; war is rapacity and bloodthirstiness while peace is beneficence and humaneness; war is an appurtenance of the world of nature while peace is of the foundation of the religion of God; war is darkness upon darkness while peace is heavenly light; war is the destroyer of the edifice of mankind while peace is the everlasting life of the world of humanity; war is like a devouring wolf while peace is like the angels of heaven; war is the struggle for existence while peace is mutual aid and cooperation among the peoples of the world and the cause of the good pleasure of the True One in the heavenly realm.

There is not one soul whose conscience does not testify that in this day there is no more important matter in the world than that of universal peace. . . .

But the wise souls who are aware of the essential relationships emanating from the realities of things consider that one single matter cannot, by itself, influence the human reality as it ought and should, for until the minds of men become united, no important matter can be accomplished. At present universal peace is a matter of great importance, but unity of conscience is

essential, so that the foundation of this matter may
become secure, its establishment firm and its edifice
strong.   2

The unity which is productive of unlimited results is
first a unity of mankind which recognizes that all
are sheltered beneath the overshadowing glory of the
All-Glorious, that all are servants of one God; for all
breathe the same atmosphere, live upon the same earth,
move beneath the same heavens, receive effulgence from
the same sun and are under the protection of one God.
This is the most great unity, and its results are lasting if
humanity adheres to it; but mankind has hitherto violat-
ed it, adhering to sectarian or other limited unities
such as racial, patriotic or unity of self-interests; therefore, no great results have been forthcoming. . . .
    Another unity is the spiritual unity which emanates
from the breaths of the Holy Spirit. This is greater than
the unity of mankind. Human unity or solidarity may be
likened to the body, whereas unity from the breaths of
the Holy Spirit is the spirit animating the body. This
is perfect unity.   3

Note ye how easily, where unity existeth in a given
family, the affairs of that family are conducted; what
progress the members of that family make, how they
prosper in the world. Their concerns are in order; they
enjoy comfort and tranquillity; they are secure; their
position is assured; they come to be envied by all. Such a
family but addeth to its stature and its lasting honor, as
day succeedeth day. And if we widen out the sphere
of unity a little to include the inhabitants of a village
who seek to be loving and united, who associate with and
are kind to one another, what great advances they will
be seen to make, how secure and protected they will be.
Then let us widen out the sphere a little more; let us take
the inhabitants of a city, all of them together: If they
establish the strongest bonds of unity among themselves,

how far they will progress, even in a brief period, and
what power they will exert. And if the sphere of unity be
still further widened out, that is, if the inhabitants of a
whole country develop peaceable hearts, and if with
all their hearts and souls they yearn to cooperate with
one another and to live in unity, and if they become kind
and loving to one another, that country will achieve
undying joy and lasting glory. Peace will it have, and
plenty, and vast wealth.

Note then: If every clan, tribe, community, every
nation, country, territory on earth should come together
under the single-hued pavilion of the oneness of mankind, and by the dazzling rays of the Sun of Truth should
proclaim the universality of man; if they should cause
all nations and all creeds to open wide their arms to one
another, establish a World Council, and proceed to
bind the members of society one to another by strong
mutual ties, what would happen then? There is no doubt
whatsoever that the divine Beloved, in all His endearing
beauty, and with Him a massive host of heavenly
confirmations and human blessings and bestowals, would
appear in His full glory before the assemblage of the
world.

Wherefore, O ye beloved of the Lord, bestir yourselves; do all in your power to be as one, to live in peace,
each with the others: For ye are all the drops from but
one ocean, the foliage of one tree, the pearls from a
single shell, the flowers and sweet herbs from the same
one garden. And achieving that, strive ye to unite the
hearts of those who follow other faiths.   4

Prejudice—The Cause of War

YE OBSERVE how the world is divided against itself,
how many a land is red with blood and its very dust
is caked with human gore. The fires of conflict have
blazed so high that never in early times, not in the
Middle Ages, not in recent centuries hath there ever

been such a hideous war, a war that is even as millstones, taking for grain the skulls of men. Nay, even worse, for flourishing countries have been reduced to rubble, cities have been leveled with the ground, and many a once prosperous village hath been turned into ruin. Fathers have lost their sons, and sons their fathers. Mothers have wept away their hearts over dead children. Children have been orphaned, women left to wander, vagrants without a home. From every aspect, humankind hath sunken low. Loud are the piercing cries of fatherless children; loud the mothers' anguished voices, reaching to the skies.

And the breeding ground of all these tragedies is prejudice: prejudice of race and nation, of religion, of political opinion; and the root cause of prejudice is blind imitation of the past—imitation in religion, in racial attitudes, in national bias, in politics. So long as this aping of the past persisteth, just so long will the foundations of the social order be blown to the four winds, just so long will humanity be continually exposed to direst peril.   5

God created one earth and one mankind to people it. Man has no other habitation, but man himself has come forth and proclaimed imaginary boundary lines and territorial restrictions, naming them Germany, France, Russia, etc. And torrents of precious blood are spilled in defense of these imaginary divisions of our one human habitation, under the delusion of a fancied and limited patriotism.

After all, a claim and title to territory or native land is but a claim and attachment to the dust of earth. We live upon this earth for a few days and then rest beneath it forever. So it is our graveyard eternally. Shall man fight for the tomb which devours him, for his eternal sepulcher? What ignorance could be greater than this? To fight over his grave, to kill another for his grave! What heedlessness! What a delusion!   6

And among the teachings of Bahá'u'lláh is that religious, racial, political, economic and patriotic prejudices destroy the edifice of humanity. As long as these prejudices prevail, the world of humanity will not have rest. For a period of six thousand years history informs us about the world of humanity. During these six thousand years the world of humanity has not been free from war, strife, murder and bloodthirstiness. In every period war has been waged in one country or another, and that war was due to either religious prejudice, racial prejudice, political prejudice or patriotic prejudice. It has, therefore, been ascertained and proved that all prejudices are destructive of the human edifice. As long as these prejudices persist, the struggle for existence must remain dominant, and bloodthirstiness and rapacity continue. Therefore, even as was the case in the past, the world of humanity cannot be saved from the darkness of nature and cannot attain illumination except through the abandonment of prejudices and the acquisition of the morals of the kingdom.   7

Attaining World Peace through the Power of God

THE establishment of peace is unachievable save through the power of the Word of God.   8

Note thou: Could these fevers in the world of the mind, these fires of war and hate, of resentment and malice among the nations, this aggression of peoples against peoples, which have destroyed the tranquillity of the whole world, ever be made to abate, except through the living waters of the teachings of God? No, never!

And this is clear: A power above and beyond the powers of nature must needs be brought to bear, to change this black darkness into light, and these hatreds and resentments, grudges and spites, these endless wrangles and wars, into fellowship and love amongst all

the peoples of the earth. This power is none other
than the breathings of the Holy Spirit and the mighty
inflow of the Word of God.   9

The Inevitability of Unity

IN CYCLES gone by, though harmony was established,
yet, owing to the absence of means, the unity of all
mankind could not have been achieved. Continents
remained widely divided, nay even among the peoples of
one and the same continent association and interchange
of thought were well-nigh impossible. Consequently,
intercourse, understanding and unity amongst all the
peoples and kindreds of the earth were unattainable. In
this day, however, means of communication have
multiplied, and the five continents of the earth have
virtually merged into one. And for everyone it is now
easy to travel to any land, to associate and exchange
views with its peoples, and to become familiar, through
publications, with the conditions, the religious beliefs
and the thoughts of all men. In like manner all the
members of the human family, whether peoples or governments, cities or villages, have become increasingly
interdependent. For none is self-sufficiency any longer
possible, inasmuch as political ties unite all peoples and
nations, and the bonds of trade and industry, of agriculture and education, are being strengthened every day.
Hence the unity of all mankind can in this day be
achieved. Verily, this is none other but one of the wonders of this wondrous age, this glorious century. Of this,
past ages have been deprived, for this century—the
century of light—hath been endowed with unique and
unprecedented glory, power and illumination. Hence the
miraculous unfolding of a fresh marvel every day. Eventually, it will be seen how bright its candles will burn
in the assemblage of man.

Behold how its light is now dawning upon the world's
darkened horizon. The first candle is unity in the politi-

cal realm, the early glimmerings of which can now be discerned. The second candle is unity of thought in world undertakings, the consummation of which will erelong be witnessed. The third candle is unity in freedom, which will surely come to pass. The fourth candle is unity in religion, which is the cornerstone of the foundation itself, and which, by the power of God, will be revealed in all its splendor. The fifth candle is the unity of nations—a unity which in this century will be securely established, causing all the peoples of the world to regard themselves as citizens of one common fatherland. The sixth candle is unity of races, making of all that dwell on earth peoples and kindreds of one race. The seventh candle is unity of language, i.e., the choice of a universal tongue in which all peoples will be instructed and converse. Each and every one of these will inevitably come to pass, inasmuch as the power of the kingdom of God will aid and assist in their realization. 10

A Call to Humanity

O PEOPLES of the world! The Sun of Truth hath risen to illumine the whole earth, and to spiritualize the community of man. Laudable are the results and the fruits thereof, abundant the holy evidences deriving from this grace. This is mercy unalloyed and purest bounty; it is light for the world and all its peoples; it is harmony and fellowship, and love and solidarity; indeed, it is compassion and unity, and the end of foreignness; it is the being at one, in complete dignity and freedom, with all on earth.

The Blessed Beauty* saith, "Ye are all the fruits of one tree, the leaves of one branch." Thus hath He likened this world of being to a single tree, and all its peoples to the leaves thereof, and the blossoms and fruits. It is needful for the bough to blossom, and leaf and fruit to

---

*Bahá'u'lláh.

flourish, and upon the interconnection of all parts of the world-tree dependeth the flourishing of leaf and blossom, and the sweetness of the fruit.

For this reason must all human beings powerfully sustain one another and seek for everlasting life; and for this reason must the lovers of God in this contingent world become the mercies and the blessings sent forth by that clement King of the seen and unseen realms. Let them purify their sight and behold all humankind as leaves and blossoms and fruits of the tree of being. Let them at all times concern themselves with doing a kindly thing for one of their fellows, offering to someone love, consideration, thoughtful help. Let them see no one as their enemy, or as wishing them ill, but think of all humankind as their friends, regarding the alien as an intimate, the stranger as a companion, staying free of prejudice, drawing no lines.

In this day, the one favored at the Threshold of the Lord is he who handeth round the cup of faithfulness, who bestoweth, even upon his enemies, the jewel of bounty, and lendeth, even to his fallen oppressor, a helping hand; it is he who will, even to the fiercest of his foes, be a loving friend. These are the teachings of the Blessed Beauty, these the counsels of the Most Great Name.

O ye dear friends! The world is at war, and the human race is in travail and mortal combat. The dark night of hate hath taken over, and the light of good faith is blotted out. The peoples and kindreds of the earth have sharpened their claws, and are hurling themselves one against the other. It is the very foundation of the human race that is being destroyed. It is thousands of households that are vagrant and dispossessed, and every year seeth thousands upon thousands of human beings weltering in their lifeblood on dusty battlefields. The tents of life and joy are down. The generals practice their general-ship, boasting of the blood they shed, competing one with the next in inciting to violence. "With this sword,"

saith one of them, "I beheaded a people!" And another:
"I toppled a nation to the ground!" And yet another:
"I brought a government down!" On such things do men
pride themselves, in such do they glory! Love—righteousness—these are everywhere censured, while despised
are harmony, and devotion to the truth.

The Faith of the Blessed Beauty is summoning mankind to safety and love, to amity and peace; it hath raised
up its tabernacle on the heights of the earth, and directeth its call to all nations. Wherefore, O ye who are
God's lovers, know ye the value of this precious Faith,
obey its teachings, walk in this road that is drawn
straight, and show ye this way to the people. Lift up your
voices and sing out the song of the kingdom. Spread far
and wide the precepts and counsels of the loving Lord, so
that this world will change into another world, and this
darksome earth will be flooded with light, and the
dead body of mankind will arise and live; so that every
soul will ask for immortality, through the holy breaths of
God.

Soon will your swiftly passing days be over, and the
fame and riches, the comforts, the joys provided by this
rubbish heap, the world, will be gone without a trace.
Summon ye, then, the people to God, and invite humanity to follow the example of the Company on high. Be
ye loving fathers to the orphan, and a refuge to the
helpless, and a treasury for the poor, and a cure for the
ailing. Be ye the helpers of every victim of oppression,
the patrons of the disadvantaged. Think ye at all times of
rendering some service to every member of the human
race. Pay ye no heed to aversion and rejection, to disdain,
hostility, injustice: Act ye in the opposite way. Be ye
sincerely kind, not in appearance only. Let each one of
God's loved ones center his attention on this: to be
the Lord's mercy to man; to be the Lord's grace. Let him
do some good to every person whose path he crosseth,
and be of some benefit to him. Let him improve the
character of each and all, and reorient the minds of men.

In this way, the light of divine guidance will shine
forth, and the blessings of God will cradle all mankind:
For love is light, no matter in what abode it dwelleth;
and hate is darkness, no matter where it may make
its nest. O friends of God! That the hidden Mystery may
stand revealed, and the secret essence of all things may
be disclosed, strive ye to banish that darkness forever and
ever.   11

16

The Day in Which We Live

A New Life for Humanity

A NEW life is, in this age, stirring within all the peoples of the earth; and yet none hath discovered its cause or perceived its motive. 1

This is the Day whereon the Ocean of God's mercy hath been manifested unto men, the Day in which the Daystar of His loving kindness hath shed its radiance upon them, the Day in which the clouds of His bountiful favor have overshadowed the whole of mankind. Now is the time to cheer and refresh the downcast through the invigorating breeze of love and fellowship, and the living waters of friendliness and charity. 2

This illumined century needeth and calleth for its fulfillment. In every century a particular and central theme is, in accordance with the requirements of that century, confirmed by God. In this illumined age that which is confirmed is the oneness of the world of humanity. Every soul who serveth this oneness will undoubtedly be assisted and confirmed. 3

Praise be to God! The medieval ages of darkness have passed away, and this century of radiance has dawned, this century wherein the reality of things is becoming evident, wherein science is penetrating the mysteries of the universe, the oneness of the world of humanity is being established, and service to mankind is the

paramount motive of all existence. Shall we remain
steeped in our fanaticisms and cling to our prejudices? Is
it fitting that we should still be bound and restricted by
ancient fables and superstitions of the past, be handi-
capped by superannuated beliefs and the ignorances of
dark ages, waging religious wars, fighting and shedding
blood, shunning and anathematizing each other? Is
this becoming? Is it not better for us to be loving and
considerate toward each other? Is it not preferable
to enjoy fellowship and unity, join in anthems of praise
to the most high God and extol all His Prophets in
the spirit of acceptance and true vision? Then, indeed,
this world will become a paradise, and the promised Day
of God will dawn. Then, according to the prophecy of
Isaiah, the wolf and the lamb will drink from the same
stream, the owl and the vulture will nest together in the
same branches, and the lion and the calf pasture in the
same meadow. What does this mean? It means that fierce
and contending religions, hostile creeds and divergent
beliefs will reconcile and associate, notwithstanding
their former hatreds and antagonism. Through the
liberalism of human attitude demanded in this radiant
century they will blend together in perfect fellowship
and love. This is the spirit and meaning of Isaiah's words.
There will never be a day when this prophecy will
come to pass literally, for these animals by their natures
cannot mingle and associate in kindness and love. Therefore, this prophecy symbolizes the unity and agreement
of races, nations and peoples who will come together
in attitudes of intelligence, illumination and spirituality.

The age has dawned when human fellowship will
become a reality.

The century has come when all religions shall be
unified.

The dispensation is at hand when all nations shall
enjoy the blessings of international peace.

The cycle has arrived when racial prejudice will be

abandoned by tribes and peoples of the world.

The epoch has begun wherein all native lands will be conjoined in one great human family.

For all mankind shall dwell in peace and security beneath the shelter of the great tabernacle of the one living God.   4

The powers of earth cannot withstand the privileges and bestowals which God has ordained for this great and glorious century. It is a need and exigency of the time. Man can withstand anything except that which is divinely intended and indicated for the age and its requirements.   5

Today the call of the kingdom is the magnetic power which draweth to itself the world of mankind, for capacity in men is great. Divine teachings constitute the spirit of this age, nay, rather, the sun of this age. Every soul must endeavor that the veils that cover men's eyes may be torn asunder and that instantly the sun may be seen and that heart and sight may be illumined thereby.   6

Therefore, it is our duty in this radiant century to investigate the essentials of divine religion, seek the realities underlying the oneness of the world of humanity and discover the source of fellowship and agreement which will unite mankind in the heavenly bond of love. 7

The Value of This Day

DO YOU appreciate the Day in which you live? This is the century of the Blessed Perfection! This is the cycle of the light of His beauty! This is the consummate day of all the prophets! These are the days of seed sowing. These are the days of tree planting. The bountiful bestowals of God are successive. He who sows a seed in this day will behold his reward in the fruits and harvest of the heavenly kingdom. This timely seed, when planted in the hearts of the beloved of God, will be watered by showers of divine mercy and warmed by the sunshine of divine love. Its fruitage and flower shall be the solidarity of mankind, the perfection of justice and the praiseworthy attributes of heaven manifest in humanity. All who sow such a seed and plant such a tree according to the teachings of Bahá'u'lláh shall surely witness this divine outcome in the degrees of its perfection and will attain unto the good pleasure of the Merciful One.   8

Know thou the value of these days; let not this chance escape thee. Beg thou God to make thee a lighted candle, so that thou mayest guide a great multitude through this darksome world.   9

The portals of His blessings are opened wide, and His signs are published abroad, and the glory of truth is blazing forth; inexhaustible are the blessings. Know ye the value of this time. Strive ye with all your hearts, raise up your voices and shout, until this dark world be filled with light, and this narrow place of shadows be widened out, and this dust heap of a fleeting moment be changed into a mirror for the eternal gardens of heaven, and this globe of earth receive its portion of celestial grace.   10

The Divine Remedy for Today

O THOU seeker after the kingdom! Every divine Manifestation is the very life of the world, and the skilled Physician of each ailing soul. The world of man is sick, and that competent Physician knoweth the cure, arising as He doth with teachings, counsels and admonishments that are the remedy for every pain, the healing balm to every wound. It is certain that the wise physician can diagnose his patient's needs at any season, and apply the cure. Wherefore, relate thou the teachings of the Abhá Beauty* to the urgent needs of this present day, and thou wilt see that they provide an instant remedy for the ailing body of the world. Indeed, they are the elixir that bringeth eternal health.

The treatment ordered by wise physicians of the past, and by those that follow after, is not one and the same; rather doth it depend on what aileth the patient; and although the remedy may change, the aim is always to bring the patient back to health. In the dispensations gone before, the feeble body of the world could not withstand a rigorous or powerful cure. For this reason did Christ say, "I have yet many things to say unto you, matters needing to be told, but ye cannot bear to hear them now. Howbeit when that Comforting Spirit, Whom the Father will send, shall come, He will make plain unto you the truth." **11**

Humanity's Role in Renewing Society

O YE lovers of God! The world is even as a human being who is diseased and impotent, whose eyes can see no longer, whose ears have gone deaf, all of whose powers are corroded and used up. Wherefore must the friends of God be competent physicians who, following the holy teachings, will nurse this patient back to health. Perhaps, God willing, the world will mend, and become permanently whole, and its exhausted faculties will be restored, and its person will take on such vigor, freshness and verdancy that it will shine out with comeliness and grace.

The first remedy of all is to guide the people aright, so that they will turn themselves unto God, and listen to His counselings, and go forth with hearing ears and seeing eyes. Once this speedily effective draught is given them, then, in accordance with the teachings, they

---

*Bahá'u'lláh.

must be led to acquire the characteristics and the behavior of the Concourse on high, and encouraged to seek out all the bounties of the Abhá Realm.* They must cleanse their hearts from even the slightest trace of hatred and spite, and they must set about being truthful and honest, conciliatory and loving to all humankind—so that East and West will, even as two lovers, hold each other close; that hatred and hostility will perish from the earth, and universal peace be firmly rooted in their place.

O ye lovers of God! Be kind to all peoples; care for every person; do all ye can to purify the hearts and minds of men; strive ye to gladden every soul. To every meadow be a shower of grace, to every tree the water of life; be as sweet musk to the sense of humankind, and to the ailing be a fresh, restoring breeze. Be pleasing waters to all those who thirst, a careful guide to all who have lost their way; be father and mother to the orphans; be loving sons and daughters to the old; be an abundant treasure to the poor. Think ye of love and good fellowship as the delights of heaven; think ye of hostility and hatred as the torments of hell.

Indulge not your bodies with rest, but work with all your souls, and with all your hearts cry out and beg of God to grant you His succor and grace. Thus may ye make this world the Abhá Paradise, and this globe of earth the parade ground of the realm on high. If only ye exert the effort, it is certain that these splendors will shine out, these clouds of mercy will shed down their rain, these life-giving winds will rise and blow, this sweet-smelling musk will be scattered far and wide. 12

O people of God! Do not busy yourselves in your own concerns; let your thoughts be fixed upon that which will rehabilitate the fortunes of mankind and sanctify the hearts and souls of men. This can best be achieved through pure and holy deeds, through a virtuous life and

---

*The kingdom of God. *Abhá* means "Most Glorious."

a goodly behavior. Valiant acts will ensure the triumph of this Cause, and a saintly character will reinforce its power. Cleave unto righteousness, O people of Bahá!* This, verily, is the commandment which this Wronged One hath given unto you, and the first choice of His unrestrained Will for every one of you. 13

A good character is, verily, the best mantle for men from God. With it He adorneth the temples of His loved ones. By My life! The light of a good character surpasseth the light of the sun and the radiance thereof. Whoso attaineth unto it is accounted as a jewel among men. The glory and the upliftment of the world must needs depend upon it. A goodly character is a means whereby men are guided to the Straight Path and are led to the Great Announcement. Well is it with him who is adorned with the saintly attributes and character of the Concourse on high. 14

The fruits of the tree of man have ever been and are goodly deeds and a praiseworthy character. Withhold not these fruits from the heedless. If they be accepted, your end is attained, and the purpose of life achieved. If not, leave them in their pastime of vain disputes. Strive, O people of God, that haply the hearts of the divers kindreds of the earth may, through the waters of your forbearance and loving kindness, be cleansed and sanctified from animosity and hatred, and be made worthy and befitting recipients of the splendors of the Sun of Truth. 15

Breathe ye into the world's worn and wasted body the fresh breath of life, and in the furrows of every region sow ye holy seed. 16

Let all your striving be for this, to become the source of life and immortality, and peace and comfort and joy, to

---

*Bahá'ís, followers of Bahá'u'lláh.

every human soul, whether one known to you or a
stranger, one opposed to you or on your side. Look ye
not upon the purity or impurity of his nature: Look
ye upon the all-embracing mercy of the Lord, the light
of Whose grace hath embosomed the whole earth and all
who dwell thereon, and in the plenitude of Whose
bounty are immersed both the wise and the ignorant.
Stranger and friend alike are seated at the table of His
favor. Even as the believer, the denier who turneth away
from God doth at the same time cup his hands and drink
from the sea of His bestowals.

It behooveth the loved ones of the Lord to be the signs
and tokens of His universal mercy and the embodiments
of His own excelling grace. Like the sun, let them cast
their rays upon garden and rubbish heap alike, and even
as clouds in spring, let them shed down their rain upon
flower and thorn. Let them seek but love and faithfulness;
let them not follow the ways of unkindness; let their
talk be confined to the secrets of friendship and of peace.
Such are the attributes of the righteous; such is the
distinguishing mark of those who serve His Threshold.   17

O ye spiritual friends! Such must be your constancy
that should the evil-wishers put every believer to death
and only one remain, that one, singly and alone, will
withstand all the peoples of the earth, and will go
on scattering far and wide the sweet and holy fragrances
of God.   18

O ye beloved of the Lord! Beware, beware, lest ye
hesitate and waver. Let not fear fall upon you, neither be
troubled nor dismayed. Take ye good heed lest this
calamitous day slacken the flames of your ardor, and
quench your tender hopes. Today is the day for steadfastness and constancy. Blessed are they that stand firm and
immovable as the rock and brave the storm and stress
of this tempestuous hour. They, verily, shall be the
recipients of God's grace; they, verily, shall receive His

divine assistance, and shall be truly victorious. They shall shine amidst mankind with a radiance which the dwellers of the Pavilion of Glory laud and magnify.   **19**

The source of courage and power is the promotion of the Word of God, and steadfastness in His Love.   **20**

Look ye not upon the fewness of thy numbers; rather, seek ye out hearts that are pure. One consecrated soul is preferable to a thousand other souls. If a small number of people gather lovingly together, with absolute purity and sanctity, with their hearts free of the world, experiencing the emotions of the kingdom and the powerful magnetic forces of the divine, and being at one in their happy fellowship, that gathering will exert its influence over all the earth. The nature of that band of people, the words they speak, the deeds they do, will unleash the bestowals of Heaven, and provide a foretaste of eternal bliss.   **21**

Look ye not upon the present; fix your gaze upon the times to come. In the beginning, how small is the seed, yet in the end it is a mighty tree. Look ye not upon the seed; look ye upon the tree, and its blossoms, and its leaves and its fruits. Consider the days of Christ, when none but a small band followed Him; then observe what a mighty tree that seed became; behold ye its fruitage. And now shall come to pass even greater things than these, for this is the summons of the Lord of Hosts, this is the trumpet call of the living Lord; this is the anthem of world peace; this is the standard of righteousness and trust and understanding raised up among all the variegated peoples of the globe; this is the splendor of the Sun of Truth, this is the holiness of the spirit of God Himself. This most powerful of dispensations will encompass all the earth, and beneath its banner will all peoples gather and be sheltered together. Know then the vital import of this tiny seed that the true Husbandman hath, with the hands of His mercy, sown in the ploughed fields of the Lord, and watered with the rain of bestowals and bounties and is now nurturing in the heat and light of the Daystar of Truth.

Wherefore, O ye loved ones of God, offer up thanks unto Him, since He hath made you the object of such bounties, and the recipients of such gifts. Blessed are ye, glad tidings to you, for this abounding grace. 22

References

References

Abbreviations Used

ABC   *'Abdu'l-Bahá in Canada,* 1962

ABL   *'Abdu'l-Bahá in London: Addresses and Notes of Conversations,*
       new ed., 1982

ADJ   *The Advent of Divine Justice,* new ed., 1984

BE   *Bahá'í Education: A Compilation,* 1977

BMFL   *Bahá'í Marriage and Family Life: Selections from the Writings of
       the Bahá'í Faith,* 1983

BNE   *Bahá'u'lláh and the New Era: An Introduction to the Bahá'í
       Faith,* 5th rev. ed., 1980

BP   *Bahá'í Prayers: A Selection of Prayers Revealed by Bahá'u'lláh,
       the Báb, and 'Abdu'l-Bahá,* new ed., 1985

BYB   *Bahá'í Year Book: Volume One—April, 1925–April, 1926,*
       1926, repr. 1980

CH   *The Chosen Highway,* n.d.; repr. 1975

ESW   *Epistle to the Son of the Wolf,* new ed., 1953

GWB   *Gleanings from the Writings of Bahá'u'lláh,* 2d ed., 1976

HWA   *The Hidden Words of Bahá'u'lláh* (Arabic), 1939; repr. 1982

HWP   *The Hidden Words of Bahá'u'lláh* (Persian), 1939; repr. 1982

KI   *Kitáb-i-Íqán: The Book of Certitude,* 2d ed., 1950

NT   New translation provided by the Universal House of Justice

OGMG   *O God, My God . . . : Bahá'í Prayers and Tablets for Children
       and Youth,* 1984

PM   *Prayers and Meditations,* 1938

PT   *Paris Talks: Addresses Given by 'Abdu'l-Bahá in Paris in 1911,*
       11th ed., 1969

PUP   *The Promulgation of Universal Peace: Talks Delivered by
       'Abdu'l-Bahá during His Visit to the United States and Canada
       in 1912,* 2d ed., 1982

SAQ   *Some Answered Questions,* 5th ed., 1981

SDC   *The Secret of Divine Civilization,* 3d ed., 1975

SF   *Spiritual Foundations: Prayer, Meditation, and the Devotional
       Attitude,* 1980

SW   *Star of the West,* vols. 7, 8
SWAB   *Selections from the Writings of 'Abdu'l-Bahá,* 1978
SWB   *Selections from the Writings of the Báb,* 1976
TAB   *Tablets of Abdul-Baha Abbas,* 3 vols., 1909–16
TB   *Tablets of Bahá'u'lláh Revealed after the Kitáb-i-Aqdas,* 1978
TN   *A Traveler's Narrative Written to Illustrate the Episode of the
        Báb,* 1980

1   Trusting in God

1 PT 108	8 PT 110–11	15 SWAB 186–87
2 SWAB 182	9 SWAB 177–78	16 SWB 177
3 NT TAB 190	10 SWAB 205	17 SWB 193
4 TAB 200	11 SWAB 51	18 BP 144
5 TAB 170	12 PUP 48	19 BP 131–32
6 TAB 158	13 PM 253–54	
7 TB 155	14 GWB 68–69	

2   Learning to Know and Love God

1 SAQ 300–01	8 PUP 293	15 HWA 9
2 PT 180–81	9 GWB 320	16 SWAB 178
3 GWB 65	10 GWB 18	17 SWAB 202–03
4 GWB 65–67	11 PUP 256–57	18 BP 153–54
5 SAQ 222	12 TB 155	19 BP 153
6 TB 144–45	13 GWB 325–26	
7 TB 268	14 HWA 4	

3   Growing through the Worlds of God

1 HWA 12	13 HWP 42	25 PT 111
2 PUP 69–70	14 SWAB 191	26 PUP 335
3 SWAB 190	15 SAQ 242–43	27 SDC 23–24
4 PT 60	16 SWB 192	28 BYB 1:43
5 SAQ 236	17 SWAB 35	29 PUP 336
6 SWAB 206	18 SWAB 33–34	30 TB 257
7 BP 4	19 SWAB 18–19	31 SWAB 271
8 GWB 70	20 PUP 334–35	32 HWA 31
9 PT 177	21 HWA 33	33 SWAB 204–05
10 PUP 225–26	22 HWA 36	34 TB 156
11 PUP 58–59	23 SW 7:163	35 SWAB 234
12 HWP 11	24 TAB 673–74	

4   *The Realm of Immortality*

1 GWB 158–59
2 GWB 161
3 GWB 141
4 SAQ 223
5 SAQ 224–25
6 HWA 14
7 SAQ 228

8   ABL 95–96
9   GWB 345
10 HWA 33
11 GWB 171
12 SWAB 177
13 SWAB 170–71
14 BNE 190

15 SAQ 232
16 PUP 47–48
17 SWAB 199–200
18 SWAB 200–01
19 BP 45–46
20 BP 46–47

5   *Prayer and Meditation*

1   SWAB 202
2   SWAB 96
3   GWB 294–95
4   SF 4
5   BNE 92–93
6   BNE 94
7   TAB 683–84
8   GWB 295
9   HWA 43
10 HWP 8
11 GWB 323
12 SWAB 79
13 TB 155
14 SWB 93–94
15 SWB 77–78

16 SWAB 202
17 GWB 265
18 SF 9
19 SF 7
20 TB 24
21 PT 61
22 BP 164
23 BP 72
24 SW 8:47
25 SWB 94
26 TAB 277
27 SAQ 231
28 PUP 246–47
29 TAB 483
30 NT TAB 426

31 GWB 303
32 PUP 187–89
33 PUP 236–37
34 PM 240
35 SWB 173
36 PM 272
37 PM 90
38 BP iii
39 KI 238
40 PT 175–76
41 PUP 459–60
42 SF 1
43 GWB 343
44 NT TAB 85

6   *Faith and Certitude*

1 TAB 62
2 GWB 86–87
3 BP 16
4 PUP 337
5 TAB 549

6   TB 156
7   BYB 1:12
8   GWB 141
9   TAB 166
10 TAB 234

11 BP 211–12
12 NT TAB 168
13 GWB 267
14 GWB 105–06
15 GWB 143

7   *Detachment and Sacrifice*

1 TB 155
2 HWA 15
3 SWAB 186
4 HWP 31

5 GWB 118
6 HWP 40
7 CH 166
8 HWA 7

9   HWA 8
10 HWP 50
11 BYB 1:42
12 GWB 276

13 SWAB 180
14 SWAB 245
15 TAB 354
16 PUP 451–52

17 PUP 148
18 SWAB 76
19 GWB 85–86
20 HWP 39

21 TN 64
22 KI 193–94
23 BP 58–59

8   Rectitude and Purity

1 PUP 453
2 HWP 5
3 PT 16
4 HWP 76
5 ADJ 23
6 GWB 305
7 SWAB 70–71
8 GWB 297

9 NT TAB 403–04
10 TB 37
11 HWA 2
12 GWB 250
13 ADJ 25
14 GWB 342
15 SWAB 158
16 TB 67

17 SWAB 146–47
18 NT TAB 704
19 HWA 59
20 ADJ 32
21 ADJ 33
22 PUP 53
23 SWAB 150

9   Obedience and Humility

1 TB 155
2 GWB 335–36
3 GWB 330–31
4 HWA 18
5 TB 155
6 ESW 27
7 TB 68
8 TB 27
9 TB 125
10 TB 93

11 GWB 332
12 TB 155
13 HWA 38
14 TAB 214
15 TB 64
16 HWA 42
17 GWB 7–8
18 ESW 44
19 SWAB 71–72
20 TAB 136

21 HWA 68
22 PUP 453
23 KI 193
24 GWB 314–15
25 SWAB 30
26 GWB 8
27 PM 238–39
28 PM 241
29 BP 11–12

10   Tests and Ordeals

1 NT SW 8:235
2 HWA 50
3 PT 50–51
4 PT 178
5 SWB 215
6 NT SW 8:238–39
7 SWAB 239
8 PT 179
9 NT TAB 324
10 PM 9
11 PM 77

12 TAB 265
13 GWB 329
14 SWAB 280–81
15 BNE 96
16 GWB 285
17 SWAB 238
18 ESW 24
19 GWB 106
20 SWAB 74
21 PM 136
22 PM 208

23 SWAB 26
24 BP 152
25 NT TAB 311
26 SWB 211
27 PM 23
28 BP 28
29 BP 29
30 BP 136
31 SWB 172

11 Practical Applications of the Spiritual Life

1 SWAB 3
2 PUP 54
3 SWAB 72
4 PUP 8
5 TB 64
6 SDC 4
7 PUP 469
8 TAB 61–62
9 NT TAB 658
10 TB 39
11 SWAB 126
12 TB 161–62
13 TB 51–52
14 SWAB 110

15 TB 35
16 TB 26
17 SWAB 145–46
18 PT 176–77
19 PT 81
20 TB 155
21 HWP 82
22 HWA 52
23 HWA 53
24 TB 156
25 HWP 53
26 TB 155–56
27 SDC 24–25
28 HWP 54

29 SWAB 115–16
30 GWB 202–03
31 HWA 57
32 GWB 265
33 SWAB 302
34 SWAB 115
35 TB 71
36 TB 88
37 PUP 453
38 KI 193
39 KI 193
40 HWA 29

12 Health and Healing

1 PT 109
2 SWAB 151
3 BNE 114–15
4 SAQ 257–58
5 SWAB 152–55
6 SWAB 151–52
7 SAQ 257
8 BNE 106

9 SWAB 156
10 BNE 106
11 PT 19
12 NT TAB 628–29
13 BNE 112
14 SWAB 150–51
15 SWAB 151
16 BNE 103

17 SWAB 147
18 ADJ 33
19 SWAB 150
20 BNE 108
21 TAB 305–06
22 SWAB 161–62
23 BP 87

13 Marriage and Family Life

1 SWAB 119
2 SWAB 117
3 SWAB 118
4 SWAB 122
5 SWAB 120
6 BMFL 30
7 SWAB 133
8 SWAB 126–27
9 SWAB 127

10 BNE 153
11 BE 6
12 SWAB 142
13 SWAB 129
14 SWAB 135–36
15 OGMG 1
16 OGMG 26
17 OGMG 13
18 SWAB 138

19 SWAB 126
20 BE 46
21 PUP 168
22 BMFL 47
23 BMFL 52–53
24 SAQ 231–32
25 SWB 211
26 BMFL 66
27 BMFL 67–68

14 Love and Fellowship

1 GWB 260
2 SWAB 27–28

3 PT 38
4 SWAB 260

5 SWAB 20
6 SWAB 286

7 SWAB 20–21
8 TB 35–36
9 GWB 95–96
10 SWB 129
11 SWAB 290–92
12 PT 53
13 PUP 44
14 PUP 57
15 PUP 208
16 ABC 31–32
17 PUP 171

18 SWAB 31
19 SWAB 299
20 TB 129–30
21 SWAB 278
22 PUP 156
23 SWB 56
24 SWAB 76
25 SWAB 203
26 NT TAB 505
27 SWAB 24
28 GWB 316

29 PT 15–16
30 GWB 289
31 PT 53
32 PUP 93
33 SWAB 230–31
34 SWAB 73
35 PT 29–30
36 SWAB 22
37 BP 101
38 BP 102–03

15   Peace and Unity

1 PT 108
2 SWAB 296–97
3 PUP 191
4 SWAB 279–80

5 SWAB 247
6 PUP 355
7 SWAB 299
8 SWAB 296

9 SWAB 53
10 SWAB 31–32
11 SWAB 1–3

16   The Day in Which We Live

1 GWB 196
2 GWB 7
3 SWAB 114
4 PUP 369–70
5 PUP 125
6 SWAB 310
7 PUP 144
8 PUP 8

9 SWAB 100
10 SWAB 36
11 SWAB 59
12 SWAB 244–45
13 TB 86
14 TB 36
15 ESW 26
16 SWAB 271

17 SWAB 256–57
18 SWAB 78–79
19 SWAB 17–18
20 TB 156
21 SWAB 80–81
22 SWAB 82–83

Index

Index